Close-Up

WORKBOOK

C1

Madeleine Williamson
Phillip McElmuray

NATIONAL
GEOGRAPHIC
LEARNING

CENGAGE
Learning

Close-Up C1 Workbook with Audio CD

Madeleine Williamson, Phillip McElmuray

Publisher: Gavin McLean

Development Editors: Angela Bandis and
    Kayleigh Buller

Project Manager: Bruce Nicholson

Project Editor: Amy Borthwick

Production Controller: Elaine Willis

Cover designer: Vasiliki Christoforidou

Text designer: Natasa Arsenidou

Compositor: MPS Ltd

Audio produced by Liz Hammond

Recorded and mixed at GFS-PRO Studio by
    George Flamouridis

ISBN: 978-1-4080-6191-6

National Geographic Learning
Cheriton House, North Way, Andover, Hampshire, SP10 5BE
United Kingdom

Cengage Learning is a leading provider of customized learning solutions with office locations around the globe, including Singapore, the United Kingdom, Australia, Mexico, Brazil and Japan. Locate your local office at: **international.cengage.com/region**

Cengage Learning products are represented in Canada by Nelson Education, Ltd.

Visit National Geographic Learning online at **ngl.cengage.com**

Visit our corporate website at **www.cengage.com**

Photo credits
Cover images: (front cover) (t) Drussawim Leepaisal/NGIC. (m) Wandy Gaotama/National Geographic Image Collection, a fisherman in Rawa Pening, Central Java, Indonesia; (back cover) Zoom Team/Shutterstock.

All images shutterstock: pp 3, 43 Galyna Andrushko; 3,5 JonMilnes; 4 Noam Armonn; 5 (b) Creative Travel Projects; 6 Lucian Coman; 7 Pal Teravagimov; 8 Diego Barbieri; 9 oliveromg; 10 (t) photomak, (b) Monkey Business Images; 11 mythja; 13 Mihai Simonia; 14 (t) Jaroslaw Grudzinski, (b) ecco; 15 Andresr; 20 Mircea Simu; 21 (m) 2 plus 3, (b) Goran Bogicevic; 22 Monkey Business Images; 23 David Hyde; 24 Piotr Marcinski; 25 Galyna Andrushko, Rob Hyrons (first aid kit); 26 Filip Fuxa; 27 the24studio; 28 leoks (Venice), Anibal Trejo (Brandenburg Gate Berlin), Daniel Leppens (hotel in Cannes); 29 Lightcraft Studio; 30 ostill; 31 Tatyana Vyc; 36 (t) Boris Mrdja, (b) Microstock Man; 37 (m) B. and E. Dudzinscy, (b) iodrakon; 38 bonchan; 39 Monkey Business Images; 40 travellight (fried rice, chicken jalfrezi), Elena Shashkina (burger and fries), Preto Perola (Greek salad); 42 fotostory; 45 (t) Linda Bucklin (dinosaurs), Mopic (meteorite), (bl) Mark Yuill, (br) antpkr; 46 Borislav Borisov (birds), Gareth Kirkland (river scene); 52 (t) Zolotova Sofiya, (b) Alexandra Lande (hang-gliding in Swiss Alps), 2happy (skydiver); 53 Ileysen; 54 dotstock; 55 Ondrej Penicka; 56 lenetstan; 57 Sura Nualpradid; 58 (t) lenetstan, (bl) Pichugin Dmitry, (br) Trevor kelly; 59 maxstockphoto; 60 Julia Ivantsova (boots), Tatyana Vyc (baby in car seat); 62 Angela Waye; 63 JMiks (online shopping), ronfromyork (closing down signs); 68 (t) Zheltyshev, (m) twistah, (b) Roxana Gonzalez; 69 fzd. it; 70 Nlshop; 71 Duirinish Light (Princes Street, Edinburgh), David Lochhead (Edinburgh Festival fireworks); 72 Ambient Ideas; 73 Rafael Ramirez Lee (MOMA), bruniewska (portrait); 74 Mauricio Avramow; 75 Eduard Stelmakh; 76 Nomad_Soul; 77 Pressmaster; 78 mangostock; 79 1000 Words; 84 (ml) dotshock, (mr) My Good Images, (bl) dotshock; 85 bikeriderlondon; 86 Fotokostic; 88 (bl) sainthorant daniel, (br) Corepics VOF; 89 Malota; 90 Lopatinsky Vladislav; 91 gary yim; 92 seeyou (cockroach), EugenP (mechanical bug); 93 (m) ostill, (b) Amnartk; 94 (t) PavelSvoboda, (b) photoslb com; 95 Dudarev Mikhail

Printed in Greece by Bakis SA
Print Number: 06   Print Year: 2016

Contents

1 Scaling the Heights

Reading

Read the article and answer the questions.

FOUR YOUNG RECORD BREAKERS OF 2012

2012 has been another great year for young record breakers. Here are four of the most impressive.

A Breaking records runs in the Shanghvi family, from Mumbai. When his brother, Parth, became the youngest scuba diver in the world in 2010, Krish Shanghvi, then aged only six, decided he too wanted to break a world record. It seemed appropriate to opt for the sky instead of the sea, but choosing skydiving proved less than straightforward. In India the minimum age for skydiving is 16, so Krish would have had to wait too long to fulfil his ambition. Then, after much research, the family discovered that in Slovenia there is no age restriction for skydiving, but unfortunately, Krish was too small to fit into the harness he would need to wear to make the dive. However, this did not deter them, and on May 22 2012, when Krish was only eight years old, he leapt out of a plane at an altitude of 3000 metres over Mozzel Bay in South Africa. Attached to diving instructor Henk van Wyk, in a tandem skydive, Krish first experienced an exhilarating 45-second free fall at 200 kilometres per hour before the parachute opened. There is little doubt, it was the biggest thrill of his life and now he too can display his own world record certificate as 'The World's Youngest Skydiver'.

B You won't find 16-year-old Laura Dekker's name in the *Guinness Book of World Records*, as it does not want to encourage minors to attempt dangerous feats of endurance. Nevertheless, she now holds the record for being the youngest round-the-world solo sailor. She completed her journey in January 2012 after a year alone at sea, but she claims her greatest challenge was persuading the Dutch authorities to allow her to embark on her journey in the first place. After several court cases, she was finally given the go-ahead on condition that she get a bigger boat with up-to-date equipment, that she learn how to cope with lack of sleep, how to put out fires and give herself first aid, including stitching her own wounds, and that she keep up with her school work. Having been born and brought up on a yacht until the age of five, when she first went to school in the Netherlands, Laura feels more comfortable at sea than on dry land. After her parents' divorce, she lived on a boat with her father, also a keen sailor, and has hardly ever lived in a house. During her year alone at sea, she faced many challenges, including storms, dangerous reefs, cockroach infestations, and sharks swimming around her yacht. But she persevered, arriving on the Caribbean island of St Maarten to be greeted by friends, fans and family. There were moments during her journey when she wondered what she was doing, but she was never tempted to give up. 'It's a dream, and I wanted to do it,' said Laura.

C 22-year-old Carlo Schmid has always had a passion for flying. By the time he was 18, he was a qualified private pilot with a licence to fly small aircraft. He worked in a bank during the week, but spent all his spare time flying. But everything changed when his mother died of cancer in 2010. Carlo decided to give up his job as a bank clerk and dedicate himself to flying. His ambition was to become the youngest pilot to fly around the world in 80 days, on his own, in a small aircraft. He set up a company and put together a team to organise the trip and raise funds for his adventure. High-profile sponsors included Swiss International Airlines. Carlo's aim was not only to break the world record, but also to raise money for a UNICEF educational project for girls in India. He set off in a six-seat Cessna 210 on July 22 2012 and landed back in Switzerland 80 days later, on September 29, having stopped in 21 countries and raised $50,000 for UNICEF. There were many challenges, not least difficult weather conditions – the extreme heat of the desert and icy clouds over the Arctic – and the considerable administrative problems involved in flying through so many countries. But Carlo prevailed and has proved himself to be a shining example of courage, determination and consideration for others. He has dedicated his round-the-world flight to the memory of his mother, who, despite suffering from a fear of flying, had loved flying with her son.

D The Ocean Rowing Society has confirmed that Tommy Tippetts has become the youngest male solo ocean rower in the world at the age of 22. It took Tommy 82 days to row across the Atlantic Ocean, from La Gomera in the Canary Islands to Port St Charles in Barbados. To begin with, Tommy had to contend with rough seas and 10-metre waves. Then the winds dropped which meant he wasn't getting much help being pushed towards his goal. But he set a steady routine, rowing ten hours a day, and arrived on April 12 2012, having rowed almost 5000 kilometres and raised over £15,000 for the mental health charity, Mind. Tommy wasn't brought up sailing and only took up rowing in his last year at university and, despite suffering badly from seasickness, his endurance and mental strength kept him going, which is why choosing to support Mind felt so appropriate. 'Although rowing the Atlantic Ocean is demanding physically, it is more of a mental test to keep going,' says Tommy.

In which section(s) are the following mentioned?

an irrational dread or phobia	1 ☐		
a feeling of nausea caused by motion	2 ☐		
being prevented from doing something because of age	3 ☐	4 ☐	
doing something for the sake of others	5 ☐	6 ☐	
financial support	7 ☐		
being influenced by the achievements of a family member	8 ☐		
learning a skill at a very young age	9 ☐	10 ☐	
learning a skill as an adult	11 ☐		
trouble with pests	12 ☐		

Vocabulary

A Choose the correct answers.

1 What ___ true adventurers from ordinary travellers is their yearning to go where no-one has ever been before.
   a achieves   **b** distinguishes   **c** resolves

2 Demand from the disabled community for increased mobility has resulted in a(n) ___ in wheelchair design.
   a revolution   **b** evolution   **c** assistance

3 He was known as a ___ criminal who felt no mercy for anyone.
   a selfless   **b** rash   **c** ruthless

4 You'll never get anywhere in business if you're so ___ all the time.
   a cautious   **b** confident   **c** gutsy

5 It was an incredible game. She ___ the title from her opponent in the last five minutes of play.
   a leapt   **b** pocketed   **c** snatched

6 I'm afraid Carl isn't very ___ which is why he hasn't done so well in his exams.
   a virtuous   **b** industrious   **c** noble

B Complete the sentences with the correct form of the words.

1 These days, there is little overt _____ against women in climbing circles.   **DISCRIMINATE**

2 Carissa's _____ in the world of surfing were matched by her remarkable earning power.   **ACCOMPLISH**

3 Their _____ was ultimately what ensured their success.   **PERSIST**

4 Paul overcame his fear of _____ and went on to win three medals in the winter games.   **FAIL**

5 It was only when he was an old man, looking back on his _____, that Simon allowed himself to feel any sense of pride.   **ACHIEVE**

6 A lack of sympathy and _____ on the part of the authorities finally lead to Anna's decision to leave the country.   **UNDERSTAND**

7 Her parents relented when they finally came to the _____ that Laura was more than capable of undertaking such a venture.   **REALISE**

8 I would say that _____ is one of the most important qualities for this particular job.   **ADAPT**

Scaling the Heights

C Complete the text with these words.

apprehensive breakthrough conceited defeated generations headstrong
impetuous modest positive triumphant upbeat went for it

What it means to be a Paralympian

Helen Hammer talks about what it means to be a Paralympian:

'Sometimes when I wake up in the morning I can't believe that being disabled has had such a(n) **(1)** _____ effect on my life. Before I had my amputation, I was just an ordinary teenager. I was a member of the school athletics team and I guess some people might have accused me of being **(2)** _____ because, having never been **(3)** _____ in a race, I admit I should have been a bit more **(4)** _____. When I had my accident and my leg had to be amputated, I did feel quite low at first. I was angry at myself for being so **(5)** _____ and taking such unnecessary risks. I should never have gone climbing in such bad weather. But I'm a pretty **(6)** _____ sort of person and with the help of my family I was able to conceive of a life with only one leg. My big break came when my PE teacher at school suggested I give wheelchair basketball a go. My parents were **(7)** _____ at first, fearing I might injure myself further, but being the **(8)** _____ person I am, I persuaded them to let me try. I was very lucky because I was a natural. I joined a local club and then came my **(9)** _____ when I was invited to try for the Paralympic team. I **(10)** _____ of course and when I was picked it was a dream come true. I felt **(11)** _____! I also feel lucky to be disabled in the 21st century as our opportunities are so much greater than those of previous **(12)** _____.'

D Complete the sentences with the correct form of the phrasal verbs.

blow away break through come up against fall through get ahead hang on knuckle down pull off

1 Samantha resigned once she realised she would never _____ if she stayed in her present job.
2 It was plain sailing as we didn't _____ any difficulties during the endeavour.
3 Our plans to go skiing have _____ because there isn't enough snow at the moment.
4 You mustn't give up; just _____ and you'll make it in the end.
5 Her classmates were absolutely _____ by the quality of Mary's painting.
6 Catherine really must _____ and practise her instrument if she wants to join the orchestra.
7 Henry managed to _____ the surprise party for his wife; she really was stunned.
8 It's almost impossible to _____ the glass ceiling as a woman working in an investment bank.

E Circle the correct words.

1 If we don't get the green light / signal soon, we won't be able to finish the project on time.
2 She was really timid when I knew her at school, but now she's really going successes / places.
3 You've got to wise up / down now and think about your future.
4 Brian is the best musician in his class by a mile / kilometre.
5 The journey went without a hitch / knot and we got there in plenty of time for the meeting.
6 Don't worry, Lucy will get / arrive there in the end. She just needs a little extra help with her maths.
7 Here, have a couple of painkillers. They'll do / fix the trick and your headache will soon be gone.
8 I don't think he'll be able to call you today. He's got a lot on his plate / chest at the moment.

Grammar

A Complete the sentences with the correct present form of the verb in brackets.

1 David _____ the house all weekend but he still hasn't finished. (paint)

2 The freezing point of water is 0°C, but seawater _____ at −2°C. (freeze)

3 I _____ the book you gave me. It's brilliant. (just/finish)

4 I'm really worried about Grandpa – he _____ things. (always/forget)

5 He never _____ to work as there's nowhere to park near his office. (drive)

6 I'm sorry I'm late! _____ long? (you/wait)

7 Sorry, I can't go out tonight. I _____ for an exam. (revise)

8 It's incredible! In 30 years of marriage, they _____ about anything. (never/disagree)

B Find and correct the mistakes in the sentences.

1 I'm sorry, Andrew isn't here. He's just been leaving the office. He'll be back after lunch.
_____

2 We're camping for the past couple of weeks, but now we're going to stay in a hotel for a few days.
_____

3 I just hear that I've passed my exams. I'm so happy!
_____

4 Susan hasn't been receiving her online order yet; she's still waiting for it.
_____

5 We've really looked forward to the concert. It promises to be brilliant.
_____

6 How do you get on with your project? Have you written the introduction yet?
_____

7 I'm afraid Jenny has never been handing her work in on time. She's always behind.
_____

8 Anthony always complains. I wish he'd stop!
_____

C Circle the correct words in the text.

The holiday of a lifetime

Clare and her husband, Adam, had been planning their trip to Africa for weeks. They **(1)** had decided / had been deciding to spend a few days relaxing on the beach before embarking on what they hoped would be the adventure of a lifetime. The first day had been wonderful. They'd seen elephants, giraffes, buffaloes and hyenas. But it was when night **(2)** fell / had been falling that the real adventure began. They **(3)** set up / had set up camp, made a fire and had some dinner. They decided they'd have an early night as it **(4)** was / had been a long day. They **(5)** didn't sleep / hadn't been sleeping for long when Clare suddenly woke up. She was sure she'd heard thunder, but then she realised the ground **(6)** shook / was shaking and their guide was shouting and clapping outside the tent. By now Adam and Clare **(7)** were / had been wide awake. Terrified, they unzipped their tent and peered out just as a herd of zebras **(8)** stampeded / had stampeded past them in a cloud of dust, narrowly avoiding them and their guide. 'I expect it's lions out hunting,' **(9)** explained / was explaining their guide, 'but don't worry. They won't come into our camp.' The next morning, when they got up after a long and restless night, Adam and Clare **(10)** found / had found lion prints all around their tent.

D Choose the correct answers.

1 Computers ___ much bigger and slower than they are today.
   a would be   **b** had been   **c** used to be

2 Once they ___ the decision to go, they saw no reason to delay their departure.
   a use to make   **b** had made   **c** had been making

3 It ___ snowing when we arrived at the resort.
   a was finally stopping **b** would finally stop   **c** had finally stopped

4 We ___ there were fairies at the bottom of the garden when we were children.
   a would believe   **b** were believing   **c** used to believe

5 Alice ___ confident about her chances of winning as she hadn't been training for very long.
   a hadn't felt   **b** didn't feel   **c** wouldn't feel

6 Mary ___ to work when the weather was good.
   a would always cycle **b** was always cycling **c** had always been cycling

7 Peter ___ at the bank for six years when he was made redundant.
   a worked   **b** was working   **c** had been working

8 Sonya was confident she'd do well in her exams as she ___ for weeks beforehand.
   a had revised   **b** was revising   **c** would revise

E Match the first parts of the sentences 1–8 to the second parts a–h.

1 Paul climbed Mount Kilimanjaro ☐   **a** when my friend showed up.
2 Andrea was swimming in the river ☐   **b** and sets in the west.
3 The sun rises in the east ☐   **c** when he was 17.
4 Sue had been training for months ☐   **d** for speeding on the motorway.
5 When Mark was a child, ☐   **e** when she ran her first marathon.
6 Instead of watching TV, ☐   **f** they would go for a walk after dinner.
7 I had been waiting for hours ☐   **g** his family used to go camping every year.
8 Delia was banned from driving ☐   **h** when she saw the crocodile.

Listening

You will hear two different extracts. For questions 1–4, choose the best answer, a, b or c. There are two questions for each extract.

Extract One

You hear two people on a music programme talking about a new CD.

1 What does the woman think of the singer's latest CD?
   a It's very impressive.
   b It isn't original.
   c It's unexpected.

2 What is the man's opinion?
   a The singer should go back to his roots.
   b The band are first-rate.
   c The singer should find a new direction.

Extract Two

You hear part of a radio interview with a man who has just swum across the English Channel.

3 The swimmer felt grateful because
   a people gave money for a cause.
   b he had realised a childhood dream.
   c he had accomplished something difficult

4 What was the greatest danger when he was swimming across the Channel?
   a the temperature of the water
   b the large number of vessels
   c the jellyfish

Writing

A Read the writing task below and write T (true) or F (false).

> *You have been asked to provide a reference for a friend of yours who has applied for a job as a group leader at Super Summer Camps for children between the ages of 8 and 12. The successful candidate must be over 18 and should be warm and caring, good with children, energetic and sporty and enjoy outdoor activities such as camping. Skills such as playing the guitar, painting or ceramics, as well as a certificate in First Aid, would be a distinct advantage.*
>
> *You should include information about your friend's character, their skills, their previous experience and reasons why they should be considered for this job.*

1 You don't know the person who has asked for the reference. ☐

2 You need to describe the person applying for the job and include information about their personality. ☐

3 You should include a paragraph about personality, another about skills and a third about experience. ☐

4 The style of the reference should be informal as the job involves working with children. ☐

B Read the model reference. Which phrases should begin and end the reference?

(1) _____

I am writing to recommend Alan Davies for the position of group leader at Super Summer Camps. Alan is now 18 years old and I have known him since we were at primary school together. We have been close friends for ten years now.

Alan is mature, responsible and organised. He is hardworking and fun loving with a great sense of humour. He is very popular, both in college and at his rugby club.

With regard to skills, not only is Alan a keen sportsman, excelling at rugby, football and swimming, he is also an accomplished musician, who can play the piano and the guitar. Furthermore, he is an experienced camper, having spent every summer holiday trekking and camping with his family.

Alan is the eldest of four and has a gift for entertaining young children, as is shown by the fact that he is always in great demand as a helper at children's birthday parties. Alan has done an advanced course in First Aid. He has also been involved in rugby training for children.

I believe Alan's personality, skills and experience make him an ideal candidate for the position of group leader. I have no hesitation in recommending him for the position.

(2) _____

Fred Scott

C Read and complete the writing task below.

> You have been asked to provide a reference for a friend who has applied for a job as an art instructor at Creative Camps for children between the ages of 6 and 10. The successful candidate must be over 18, should be friendly and approachable, good with children, enthusiastic and artistic, with good skills in drawing and pottery.
>
> Include information about your friend's character, skills, previous experience and reasons why they should be considered for this job.

*Write your **reference** in 220–260 words in an appropriate style.*

Watch the clock!

 Spend 5 minutes reading the task and planning your reference.

 Spend 30 minutes writing your reference.

 Spend 5 minutes checking and editing your reference.

Remember!

In a reference say who you are and how you know the person you're writing about. Include information about their character, skills and experience. Don't include information that isn't relevant to the job. Use formal language and organise your ideas into paragraphs. Use positive language and make sure you present the person in a favourable light. Don't forget to say why you think the person should be given the job. See the Writing Reference for references on page 175 of the Student's Book for further help.

Reading

Read the texts and choose the answer (a, b, c or d) which fits best according to the text.

Blogging Your Way Back to Health

Anyone who suffers compound fractures of both legs might be expected to indulge in a moment of self-pity. However, Heather McLean is not one to feel sorry for herself. Instead, the 16-year-old schoolgirl, who in April last year survived a horrific car accident, started a blog (called *Breaking News*), sharing all the successes and setbacks on her slow and often painful road to recovery. Initially, she had only a few followers, mainly family members and friends, but after appearing on a local radio phone-in where she mentioned her blog, her fame grew rapidly and she soon had thousands of subscribers.

But given that there are well over one hundred million blogs worldwide on the two main blogging platforms, it must take more than a plug on local radio to make a blog successful. So what was Heather's secret? 'Keep it interesting,' says Heather. 'People don't want to read about what you ate for lunch or what you watched on TV. But there's so much going on around you in a hospital and so many interesting people with often very dramatic and touching stories. You just have to keep your eyes and ears open.'

Not all of the attention she received was positive or supportive, however. Her blog was a frequent target for spammers (people leaving comments promoting their own commercial websites), and occasionally visitors left derogatory and sometimes hurtful comments. 'It's very easy to hide behind a username,' observes Heather. 'But you have to feel sorry for people like that. They must have very sad lives if they feel that they have to indulge in such cowardly behaviour.'

By far the biggest draw to Heather's blog – as evidenced by the comments of visitors – was her humorous and overwhelmingly positive attitude even in her darkest moments. Perhaps this comment best sums it up: 'Thank you, Heather. You are such a brave girl and an inspiration to us all.'

Facebook Addict

Dan Cole used to spend four or five hours a day on Facebook. It ruled his life. He didn't consider it a problem until he failed an important exam. 'I'd always been an A student and it was the first time I'd done badly,' explains Dan. 'My parents immediately identified the amount of time I spent on Facebook as the culprit, and I had to admit that they were right: I was a Facebook addict. So, I agreed to deactivate my account until I'd retaken and passed the exam.'

To start with, Dan felt as though his life had ended. He had relied on Facebook for everything, from organising his photo albums to arranging to meet up with friends. 'I suddenly had all this time on my hands and I didn't know what to do with it. I saw it as a negative thing rather than an advantage.' But slowly Dan's life began to resemble the one he had had pre-Facebook. He could no longer claim 432 'friends', but he kept in touch by phone with the people who were important to him. He started to read books again – and he still had time to revise for his exam. Of course, he passed with flying colours.

As soon as he got his results, Dan logged back into his Facebook account. 'I was full of anticipation. I expected to be sucked back into the world that I'd missed so much. But I soon realised that I hadn't missed anything, apart from a few updated status pages. I found myself disappointedly logging out again in less than an hour.' Dan still uses Facebook, but these days he controls it instead of it controlling him.

1 On Heather's blog you can read about
   a   the thousands of people who follow her online.
   b   her secrets for success in life.
   c   people like her with health problems.
   d   her normal, everyday activities.

2 The majority of people who read Heather's blog
   a   enjoy it because of her optimism and courage.
   b   want people to buy their products.
   c   leave messages telling her she's cowardly.
   d   want to know what she's been doing.

3 Dan temporarily switched off his Facebook account
   a   to meet up with friends in real life.
   b   so his studies wouldn't suffer.
   c   so he could spend time reading.
   d   because he didn't like social networking.

4 Once Dan reactivated his Facebook account he
   a   regained all 432 friends he thought he'd lost.
   b   stopped reading books and revising for exams.
   c   fell back into his old networking habits.
   d   no longer enjoyed it as much as he used to.

Vocabulary

A   Circle the correct words.

1   We had no choice / reaction but to cancel his club membership as he was unable to keep up with the payments.
2   Before he went abroad, Paul promised to keep in contact / access by email and texting.
3   You shouldn't divulge username / personal information on the Internet or over the phone.
4   I don't think the chat show was the appropriate platform for them to air their political contacts / views.
5   Nadia wasn't sure if it was a realistic / legitimate website, so she didn't log on.
6   Mark was very upset when he saw that Anna had updated / identified her status to 'single' after their quarrel.
7   I won't shop online because someone could steal my identity / personality when I fill in my details.
8   To download films, just tick / click on the link below and follow the instructions. It's really easy.

B   Complete the text with these words.

avoided   criticism   observed   offended   relates   remark   resist   value

Cake for breakfast

People often don't realise that a throwaway **(1)** _____ can have a profound effect, especially when it comes from a parent. The first time Carlo Russell baked a cake, his mother **(2)** _____ that it was 'quite nice, but a bit dry'. Carlo was so **(3)** _____ by what he perceived as her **(4)** _____ that he **(5)** _____ baking for years. In fact, he didn't start again until he went to college, which is quite ironic, of course, as he's best known as the man who inspired men and women all over the country to get baking again. Carlo **(6)** _____ this and many more stories about his early life in his new autobiography, *Cake for Breakfast*. He also describes his relationship with his grandmother, who inspired him to follow his dream and taught him to **(7)** _____ the simple things in life, to **(8)** _____ the temptation to settle for second best and to strive for perfection in everything he does. 'She would have been thrilled by my success,' says Carlo. 'I wish she could have seen me on TV. She would have been so impressed!'

C Complete the sentences with the correct form of the words.

1 Although Hannah finds it difficult to accept _____, she's trying not to let it upset her too much.

2 They didn't do a very good job, but in their _____, you have to admit they weren't given much time to do it.

3 After the launch of our latest smartphone, we were expecting a more positive _____ from the press.

4 The problem with this website is that it isn't _____ from mobile phones.

5 I've asked you to stop _____ your sister three times now!

6 Daniel only retaliated after extreme _____.

7 All this _____ is sure to mean the children won't be able to get to sleep tonight.

8 I read the most _____ report about identity theft on the Internet last week. It made me scared to go online!

CRITICISE

DEFEND

REACT

ACCESS

BOTHER

PROVOKE

EXCITE

SHOCK

D The words in bold are in the wrong sentences. Write each word next to the correct sentence.

1 Peter was taken **down** by the resentment his proposal to bring in a new director provoked.   _____

2 My brother has taken **for** meeting his friends for coffee before coming home after college.   _____

3 Unfortunately, the new website has come in **at** a lot of criticism because it is so user-unfriendly.   _____

4 She got back **to** him eventually when she published her autobiography and revealed his true nature to the world.   _____

5 My aunt set **aback** to do a short course in art history, but ended up doing a masters and getting a job in a museum.   _____

6 You really must learn to stop cutting **up** when I'm talking. It's terribly rude.   _____

7 What's the point in stirring things **in** now, twenty years after the event? Just leave it alone!   _____

8 Popular uprisings like this one have been known to bring **out** repressive authoritarian regimes.   _____

E Choose the correct answers.

1 I'm not sure how many people came to the conference, but I'd say, at ___, there were over 100 people there.
a a possibility   b an idea   c a guess

2 A little ___ told me it was your birthday today. Many happy returns!
a canary   b bird   c goose

3 If you take them out of ___, of course his comments will sound ridiculous.
a article   b newspaper   c context

4 He had the courage to tell her to her ___ that she was a liar.
a face   b head   c back

5 Seriously, they're moving to the US next year. I know it's true because I got it straight from the ___ mouth.
a frog's   b cat's   c horse's

6 I'm telling you this in the strictest ___ so you really mustn't repeat it to anyone.
a context   b confidence   c word

7 Alice wouldn't say ___ to a goose; she's so quiet and timid.
a boo   b hi   c hush

8 It happened without ___. One minute he had a great job, the next he was unemployed.
a telling   b announcement   c warning

Grammar

A Complete the sentences with the correct form of the verb in brackets.

1 _____ I _____ ice cream for dessert or would you rather a cake? (bring)

2 This time next year, Sarah _____ for her final exams. (revise)

3 By the end of July next year, she _____ her exams. (finish)

4 By the end of April, Tony _____ his novel for two years. When is he planning to finish it? (write)

5 I don't think Paul _____ to see you this time. He just hasn't got enough time. (manage)

6 I've finally made up my mind. I _____ for a job abroad. (look)

7 I'm so sorry, there's a mistake on the itinerary I gave you. We _____ to Miami on Thursday, not on Wednesday. (fly)

8 I'm sure we _____ the film. It's had such good reviews. (enjoy)

B Complete the texts with these verb forms.

> are going to expect   will be moving   will become   will continue
> will have peaked   will have realised   will sound   won't be able to follow

Media experts offer their thoughts on the future of social networking

*'Some people have argued that social networking **(1)** _____ by the end of the decade, but with over one billion Facebook users worldwide, it seems quite unlikely, especially if China becomes a viable market.'*

'I agree that social networking is here to stay, but I think it **(2)** _____ more private, with users opting for premium and niche networks with a limit on friends to 50 or so. In ten years' time, claiming to have 500 plus friends on Facebook **(3)** _____ superficial and out-dated.'

*'Only those sites which are compatible with mobile phones **(4)** _____ to do well. As people communicate more and more via their mobile phones, they **(5)** _____ faster and more reliable networks. Social networking is here to stay.'*

'Well, I'm not entirely sure. Social networking used to be the realm of the young, but now, as their parents join sites such as Facebook, many young people are going to be tempted to join other sites where their parents **(6)** _____. I think increasingly, kids **(7)** _____ around, finding new sites that suit them as they go to university and start their careers.'

*'Two issues will have a consequence on social networking, one is privacy and the other is addiction. People are becoming increasingly aware of what these mean in terms of their reputation and mental health and I predict that in ten or twenty years' time, people **(8)** _____ that it's in the real world they want to be living, not the virtual one. They'll still be networking, but it won't be the same. They won't be ruled by it anymore.'*

C Find and correct the mistakes in the sentences.

1 Am I going to carry your bag for you? It looks very heavy.

2 By the end of the year, Paul and Anita will marry for six months.

3 Don't worry, I'll cook dinner tonight. I go to the supermarket on my way home.

4 Look, it's here on our itinerary: we're going to have arrived on the 9th of June.

5 I'm picking John up at 3pm and then we will have driven to the coast.

6 By September, they are working on the house for over a year.

7 I've been helping you for weeks, but I don't help you anymore! You're so ungrateful.

8 I will have sunbathed on the beach this time next week. I can't wait!

D Match the first parts of the sentences 1–6 to the second parts a–f.

1 Paul decided he would buy a new smartphone ☐

2 Lisa realised it was going to be a very late night ☐

3 Sarah told her mother she would pick her up ☐

4 They saved some money when they were on holiday ☐

5 I knew it was going to snow as soon as ☐

6 They weren't going to allow her to travel ☐

a because they were staying with their aunt and uncle.

b as soon as he got his pay cheque.

c because of her condition.

d after she'd dropped the kids off at school.

e I saw the black clouds and realised how cold it had got.

f because by ten o'clock she had only written the introduction.

E Complete the second sentences so that they have a similar meaning to the first sentences. Use the words in bold.

1 Carl moved to Los Angeles in August. It's December now. **living**
By February next year, he _____ in Los Angeles for six months.

2 You mustn't be late. You really need to go now. **will**
Do you realise you _____ if you don't go now?

3 Oh, dear! At this rate Anne won't have finished tidying up by the time all the guests arrive. **still**
Anne _____ when the guests start arriving.

4 The plan is to meet up at 6pm and have a meal before going to the cinema. **meeting**
We _____ at 6pm for a meal before watching a film.

5 Listen, the minute you finish your homework, we can go to the beach. **finished**
As _____, we'll go to the beach.

6 The plan had been to meet up for a pizza, but she came down with a cold. **going**
We _____ for a pizza, but she came down with a cold.

7 They checked their equipment because they had to start their journey later that night. **starting**
They checked their equipment because _____ later that night.

8 Mark realised it was best to apply to medical school after getting his exam results. **would**
Mark decided _____ once he had got his exam results.

Listening

🔊 **You will hear someone talking about her views on an aspect of technology. For questions 1–8, complete the sentences.**

1 The speaker was concerned that digital books would eventually replace _____ books.

2 In addition to the feel and smell of paper books, the speaker has always loved their _____.

3 The speaker states that because people are increasingly reading e-books, paper books are _____ in popularity.

4 She thinks the advantages of e-books _____ the disadvantages.

5 When the speaker received an e-book reader as a present, she was _____ immediately.

6 As well as reading in _____ again, the speaker has begun to read the novels she meant to read when she was young.

7 The speaker says that _____ to newer technology is bad for the planet.

8 The speaker now only reads paper books when she is at the _____.

Writing

A Read the writing task below and tick the things you have to do.

Following a class discussion, your teacher has asked you to write an essay giving your views on this topic.

> *The increase in the use of e-book readers is likely to have a significant impact on the environment. Some people say that it is bound to be beneficial as fewer paper books will be produced. Do you agree that the advent of e-readers is good for the environment? What disadvantages are associated with e-book readers?*

1 start with an introduction ☐
2 decide if your essay should be formal or conversational ☐
3 use only present tenses in your essay ☐
4 talk about the advantages of using e-book readers ☐
5 discuss the disadvantages of using e-book readers ☐
6 finish each paragraph with a topic sentence ☐
7 give your opinion ☐
8 include linking words and phrases ☐

Remember!

In an essay your main aim is to present an argument and a clear rationale to back it up. Should it be formal or informal? What functions will you need to focus on, for example, describe a process, give your opinion, explain your rationale? Think also about the grammar and vocabulary you will be using and don't forget to organise your essay into an introduction, main body and conclusion, making sure each paragraph begins with a topic sentence. Finally, link your ideas with appropriate linking words and phrases. See the Writing Reference for essays on page 176 of the Student's Book for further help.

B Read the model essay and complete it with these words.

as a result   however   nevertheless   secondly   thirdly   though

No-one can doubt that e-books are here to stay. E-book sales have already overtaken sales of paper books in the USA, and soon the rest of the world will follow. But what impact will this have on the environment?

Optimists claim that e-books are environmentally friendly. Firstly, no paper is needed and therefore fewer trees need to be cut down. **(1)** _____, as the carbon footprint of a paperback involves paper production, printing, shipping and the destruction of at least 25% of books, which are never bought, e-books must be greener. **(2)** _____, once you have an e-reader, you can download thousands of books and read them on one device. **(3)** _____, the carbon footprint of an e-book will only involve the initial purchase of the e-reader and battery charging.

(4) _____, pessimists only need to identify the mountains of obsolete computers filling our landfill sites to set alarm bells ringing. How can e-books be more ecological, they argue, when we consider what will happen as people upgrade, buying smaller and more powerful devices to read their e-books on? Outdated e-readers will join the heaps of computers and multiply the carbon footprint of an e-book well beyond that of a conventional paperback.

I am not a pessimist, **(5)** _____. We are unlikely to return to the lending library – without doubt the most environmentally-friendly reading method of all. **(6)** _____, as people become more aware, they will find solutions to these problems. We now recycle vast quantities of old computers and hopefully we'll do the same with e-readers.

C Read and complete the writing task below.

Following a class discussion, your teacher has asked you to write an essay giving your views on this topic.

> *Many people believe that e-books will revolutionise the world of publishing as more and more individuals self-publish, doing away with the need for an editor, publisher, printer or even a conventional bookshop. Do you think this will have a detrimental effect on the quality of books being published? What do you think publishers can do to keep their businesses going?*

*Write your **essay** in 220–260 words in an appropriate style.*

Watch the clock!

 Spend 5 minutes reading the task and planning your essay.

 Spend 30 minutes writing your essay.

 Spend 5 minutes checking and editing your essay.

Vocabulary

A Choose the correct answers.

1 Amanda is rather set in her ways. She isn't very ___.
  a apprehensive
  b impetuous
  c adaptable
  d inflexible

2 These are so similar, I can't ___ between them.
  a persist
  b distinguish
  c resolve
  d realise

3 If you want to succeed, ___ high.
  a aim
  b insist
  c discriminate
  d strive

4 He was ___ in his criticism, but he was fair.
  a cunning
  b sentimental
  c reckless
  d merciless

5 Arthur isn't ___ despite his achievements.
  a candid
  b cautious
  c conceited
  d considerate

6 We came ___ against many obstacles.
  a off
  b up
  c through
  d down

7 They pulled it ___, and the concert was a success.
  a off
  b up
  c on
  d away

8 We didn't sell the house as the offer fell ___.
  a away
  b down
  c off
  d through

9 I'm exhausted. I've got too much ___ my plate.
  a in
  b at
  c on
  d by

10 Marina was ___ fire for making bad decisions.
  a in
  b on
  c under
  d by

11 Don't reveal your ___ information online.
  a personal
  b access
  c identity
  d user

12 It's not a ___ email, so don't reply to the message.
  a moral
  b impressive
  c provoked
  d legitimate

13 I was the victim of ___ theft.
  a personality
  b identity
  c character
  d link

14 Lucinda has ___ her status to 'in a relationship'.
  a remarked
  b linked
  c updated
  d related

15 Congratulations! That's such ___ news.
  a exciting
  b shocking
  c ideal
  d critical

16 Deborah was taken ___ by his harsh criticism.
  a down
  b up
  c in
  d aback

17 Their imprisonment has ___ up international outrage.
  a stirred
  b rushed
  c cut
  d backed

18 She'd never tell Theo he was boring ___ his face.
  a in
  b to
  c by
  d for

19 They set ___ to build a successful retail business.
  a off
  b out
  c to
  d up

20 A little ___ told me you passed all your exams!
  a canary
  b owl
  c cat
  d bird

Grammar

B **Choose the correct answers.**

1 Oh, no. I think I ___ my wallet at home.
  a leave
  b am leaving
  c have left
  d have been leaving

2 Is he getting enough sleep? He ___ exhausted!
  a seems
  b is seeming
  c has seemed
  d has been seeming

3 We ___ to spend the weekend in Paris. I can't wait!
  a decide
  b are deciding
  c have decided
  d will be deciding

4 Lynn ___ very well recently.
  a doesn't feel
  b isn't feeling
  c used to feel
  d hasn't been feeling

5 ___ the mail yet today? I'm waiting for a parcel.
  a Do they deliver
  b Are they delivering
  c Have they delivered
  d Have they been delivering

6 Until recently, my granny ___ for long walks.
  a have always been going
  b had always been going
  c are always going
  d would always go

7 Our postman ___ our mail for years.
  a has delivered
  b has been delivering
  c is delivering
  d would deliver

8 She ___ me a cup of tea in bed, which was so kind.
  a will bring
  b is bringing
  c brought
  d was bringing

9 The film ___ when we got to the cinema.
  a already started
  b has already started
  c had already started
  d would already be starting

10 Before becoming an artist, Doris ___ in a bank.
  a has worked
  b used to work
  c would work
  d has been working

11 Don't worry. Caroline ___ you tidy your room.
  a will help
  b would help
  c will have helped
  d has been helping

12 The show ___ by the time I turned on the TV.
  a had finished
  b has been finishing
  c will have finished
  d will have been finishing

13 Brian told me he ___ me paint the house next week.
  a will help
  b will have helped
  c will be helping
  d would help

14 By the time the cake ___ ready, the boys will be home.
  a is
  b was
  c will be
  d would be

15 ___ on holiday in June or July? What do you think?
  a Do we go
  b Would we go
  c Shall we go
  d Have we gone

16 I can't go out tomorrow. I ___ all day for my exams.
  a will have revised
  b would be revising
  c will be revising
  d will have been revising

17 He will start driving to work once he ___ his test.
  a is passing
  b will pass
  c will have passed
  d has passed

18 What are your plans? ___ football on Saturday?
  a Will you play
  b Are you going to play
  c Do you play
  d Have you played

19 My grandparents ___ for fifty years in April!
  a are married
  b had been married
  c will have been married
  d are going to be married

20 He had a feeling he ___ the race, so he didn't try.
  a wouldn't win
  b won't win
  c isn't winning
  d hasn't won

Use of English

C Choose the correct answer.

Bill Gates

The founder of Microsoft, Bill Gates, has achieved **(1)** ___ success as a computer programmer, inventor and entrepreneur. His path to that point, however, was anything but typical. While attending Harvard University in the 1970s, he made a **(2)** ___ move and left university before graduating to start his own company. His parents didn't like the idea at first, but Gates **(3)** ___ down and worked hard to get their support. He founded Microsoft in 1975, which after a few short years caused a(n) **(4)** ___ in personal computing. During the time that Gates was at the head of the company, some of his employees regarded him as **(5)** ___ and arrogant. He would sometimes **(6)** ___ in on presentations, expressing his dislike for certain ideas and proposals. He was often described as being **(7)** ___; he did whatever he liked and was often hard to reach either in or out of the office. But whatever anyone may have thought of these minor shortcomings, Gates was a **(8)** ___ competitor in the computer software industry who often **(9)** ___ the competition. In his years as CEO of the company, he laboured hard at **(10)** ___ Microsoft's range of software products, and whenever he **(11)** ___ success in a particular area of computing, Gates guarded the position with all his might. Since then, he has won international **(12)** ___ as one of the greatest computer software inventors of all time.

1	a	gruelling	b	cunning	c	crushing	d	staggering
2	a	gutsy	b	virtuous	c	candid	d	noble
3	a	broke	b	knuckled	c	fell	d	got
4	a	evolution	b	discrimination	c	generation	d	revolution
5	a	impartial	b	modest	c	mediocre	d	conceited
6	a	cut	b	break	c	put	d	come
7	a	considerate	b	candid	c	noble	d	impetuous
8	a	ruthless	b	reckless	c	worthless	d	selfless
9	a	executed	b	crushed	c	snatched	d	pocketed
10	a	growing	b	broadening	c	lengthening	d	elongating
11	a	achieved	b	defeated	c	accomplished	d	resolved
12	a	acceptance	b	approval	c	acclaim	d	applause

D Complete the text by writing one word in each gap.

Failure is the key to success

Someone once said 'Failure is the key to success; each mistake teaches us something'. Some people think success means pulling **(1)** _____ the impossible, getting **(2)** _____ in your career at all costs, and having all your endeavours succeed **(3)** _____ a hitch. But what if the above saying were true? That would mean if not a single one of our plans ever fell **(4)** _____, we wouldn't be learning a lesson along the way. As is the case for most, we've all come up **(5)** _____ problems and bad situations that happened without **(6)** _____. How many times have you gone **(7)** _____ out on an assignment, only to see it fail? Or worse, you learn that another person did better than you **(8)** _____ a mile, or you came **(9)** _____ for a lot of criticism for your own work when you thought you **(10)** _____ your best. This has happened to all of us on **(11)** _____. The trick is to hang **(12)** _____ with the same enthusiasm as you had before and you'll eventually get **(13)** _____. Try doing things differently next time and you'll find that you may just **(14)** _____ through to new discoveries about your abilities. Then one day soon, you may be blowing everyone **(15)** _____ with your tremendous success!

E Think of one word only that can be used appropriately in all three sentences.

1 If you can't gain _____ to your account, perhaps you're using the wrong password.
You're not allowed to view details on this profile because you don't have _____.
In order to _____ the file, you have to double click on the icon.

2 I'm afraid I don't have the _____ to be successful in life.
Kelly told me the secret in _____, so a secret it will remain.
Kevin is certainly not lacking in _____ and in fact may be a bit arrogant.

3 If you _____ at your password and do so wrongly, you might get locked out of your account.
At a _____, I would say they know each other through Facebook.
I don't know how to delete a profile – your _____ is as good as mine!

4 Michelle's profile picture is of her riding a _____.
Rachel told her kids not to _____ around inside the house.
I know who hacked into your account – I got it straight from the _____'s mouth!

5 Patrick posted a picture of his new home's _____ site online.
The _____ company has a Facebook page where you can learn about new projects they're building.
My blog site is still under _____, so give me a few more days to finish it.

F Complete the second sentences so that they have a similar meaning to the first sentences using the words in bold. Use between three and six words.

1 The user changed the meaning of what I said and I was quite upset about it.
CONTEXT
The user _____ and I was quite upset over it.

2 A person who puts a negative comment online usually won't tell you in person.
FACE
A person who writes something negative online usually won't _____.

3 I don't blog because my writing skills are quite lacking.
SCRATCH
Because my writing skills _____, I don't do any blogging.

4 I'm too busy to help you at the moment.
PLATE
I can't help you because I've _____ at the moment.

5 We can start the project as soon as we get the approval.
GREEN
We can start the project once we _____.

6 She thought the online comment was very surprising.
ABACK
She _____ the online comment.

7 We'll have to put in many hours to finish this assignment.
CLOCK
We'll have to _____ to finish this assignment.

8 I'm warning you not to take revenge on Neil for what he said.
BACK
I'm warning you _____ Neil for what he said.

3 Just for the Health of It

Reading

Five paragraphs have been removed from the text. Choose from the paragraphs A–F the one which fits each gap (1–5). There is one extra paragraph which you do not need to use.

Living with CFS

When she was 16, Alexa Gallo was captain of her school netball team and a keen swimmer and dancer. She would bounce out of bed in the morning and keep going until late into the evening. But by the time she was 20, she was virtually bedridden. Even the effort of walking to her bedroom door would leave her utterly exhausted and in tears. **1**

On top of the flu-like symptoms, she began to experience memory loss, very disturbed sleep and dizziness. 'It was very upsetting,' recalls Alexa. 'I had no idea what was happening to me, and my doctor couldn't explain it either.' **2**

Alexa was working part-time in a beauty salon at the time. Initially, her boss was very sympathetic and told her to take as much time as she needed to recover, but that easygoing attitude changed when Alexa was still unable to work after a month. One day she got a call to say that they couldn't keep her job open any longer and they were going to employ someone else. **3**

It wasn't only her job that she lost. As time went on, she saw less and less of her friends. 'Frankly, I think they just got bored with me. I don't blame them. They would come to visit me, but I was often too ill to see them or unable to talk to them.' In the end, most of her friends gave up coming altogether. **4**

What was the turning point? 'There wasn't a turning point as such,' says Alexa. 'There was just a gradual diminishing of the symptoms—but it was extremely gradual, and there were plenty of setbacks on the way. For example, sometimes a symptom would disappear for a while only to come back worse than before. But, at a certain point I realised there was light at the end of the tunnel.' **5**

A No ethnic or racial group is more or less likely to contract CFS, but it is more common among women than among men. In fact, between 60 and 85% of reported cases are women. However, there is some evidence to suggest that the occurrence of the disease in men is underreported. The disease is most common among 40- to 60-year-olds, with children and adolescents less likely to contract it than adults.

B 'I wasn't surprised,' says Alexa. 'And to be honest, I was much too ill to care. I knew I couldn't work anyway. Luckily, I was still living with my parents at the time, so I didn't have to pay rent or other bills. But I don't know how I would have coped if I hadn't been able to rely on my parents.'

C Today, Alexa enjoys a normal life and her CFS seems a distant memory. She is married and has two healthy children. She works out at the gym two or three times a week and goes for long family walks at the weekend. But she is one of the few lucky ones. Many people never fully recover from the disease and there is still no known cure.

D So what caused this dramatic change? At first, Alexa thought she had bad flu. She awoke one day with a severe headache, a sore throat and aching muscles. But whereas a bout of flu would have cleared up after a few days, especially in such a young, fit person, Alexa's symptoms just seemed to grow in number and worsen.

E Having lost her job and her friends, Alexa hit rock bottom. 'I honestly wished I was dead. I was in constant pain and there didn't seem to be any way out. I tried psychological therapy, physical therapy and lots of different diets, but nothing seemed to make any difference.'

F Eventually, after various scans and lots of tests, she was diagnosed with Chronic Fatigue Syndrome (CFS), a disease that causes severe tiredness and prevents the sufferer from performing normal, everyday activities. The diagnosis took a long time because the only way to be sure that a person has the disease is by eliminating all the other possible diseases that have similar symptoms.

Vocabulary

A Complete the sentences with the correct form of the words.

1 Susan had _____ feelings about taking the medication her doctor prescribed because of the unpleasant side effects.

2 Although he was seriously injured, Donald was only just conscious and seemed to be _____ to the pain.

3 It's just a _____ pain. Luckily nothing is broken.

4 Poor Grandpa. He's getting more and more _____ every day.

5 People often don't realise how important it is to eat _____ food when they're training.

6 How _____ do you think this diet will be?

7 Jilly lost too much weight on her diet and now she's really _____.

8 The _____ of the illness involves taking medicine and lots of bed rest.

MIX

OBLIVION

MUSCLE

FORGET

NUTRIENT

BENEFIT

BONE

TREAT

B Complete the text with these words.

anorexic   dehydrated   emotional   intravenous   monitored
psychological   physical   recovered   relieved   undernourished

The diagnosis

I know it sounds crazy, but I actually felt **(1)** _____ the day I was diagnosed with coeliac disease. Finally, there was a reason why I had constant stomach aches, couldn't keep my food down and kept losing weight. Having coeliac disease means you're allergic to gluten, a protein found in wheat, so no more bread or pasta for me. I realise now that it had been going on for years. My doctor had come to the conclusion that my symptoms were **(2)** _____ because I was always in such a(n) **(3)** _____ state when I saw him. He even prescribed antidepressants, but I refused to take them. I wasn't depressed; I was ill. More months went by, and as I lost more and more weight, my friends and family began to think I was **(4)** _____. But I was desperate to eat and enjoy my food. Then, after having lasagne for dinner one night, I had such

a bad reaction that I ended up in hospital, where they put me on a(n) **(5)** _____ drip because I was so **(6)** _____. And that was when the tests were finally done and they found out that it wasn't all in my head. It was a(n) **(7)** _____ illness after all. I was kept in hospital for a few days as I had become seriously **(8)** _____ – I had been sick for so long, I had a serious vitamin and mineral deficiency. Then I had to be **(9)** _____ for six months until I regained the weight I'd lost. But I've been on a gluten-free diet ever since and now I feel fantastic. I've completely **(10)** _____.

C Choose the correct answers.

1 Because it's a very deep wound, it will probably take a few months before it's completely ___.
  a recovered   **b** healed   **c** fixed

2 Anthony has got such a(n) ___ imagination that I sometimes worry he loses track of reality.
  a vivid   **b** mental   **c** alive

3 In order to produce an exact copy, you'll need ___ measurements.
  a stern   **b** proper   **c** precise

4 Veins, arteries and capillaries are all blood ___.
  a lines   **b** vessels   **c** ways

5 Because Fiona suffers from low blood ___, she often feels dizzy, especially if she gets up too quickly.
  a pressure   **b** force   **c** flow

6 There are four main blood ___: A, B, AB and O.
  a kinds   **b** varieties   **c** types

7 Luckily, nobody was seriously ___ in the accident.
  a injured   **b** damaged   **c** harming

8 Three soldiers were mortally ___ and died shortly after reaching hospital.
  a harmed   **b** wounded   **c** hurt

D The words in **bold** are in the wrong sentences. Write each word next to the correct sentence.

1 After her accident her legs were in a terrible state, with **splitting** sores that took ages to heal.   _____

2 Poor Peter had such a violent **running** fit that he threw up.   _____

3 Some **internal** functions like sneezing are very difficult to control.   _____

4 She's so old now, she has **terminal** eyesight and very poor hearing.   _____

5 The effect of obesity on people's **bodily** organs is more dangerous than its effect on their appearance.   _____

6 He was diagnosed with a **failing** illness and died within six months.   _____

7 Some psychiatrists believe that mental illness is caused by a **coughing** imbalance in the brain and that only medication can bring on a cure.   _____

8 Laura had such a **chemical** headache that she had to go to bed in a darkened room.   _____

E Match the first parts of the sentences 1–6 to the second parts a–f.

1 Karen had food poisoning ☐

2 I had to have my appendix taken out because ☐

3 The first time I watched an operation when I was at medical school, ☐

4 I avoid going to the doctor's because ☐

5 Andrew's immune system is so weak ☐

6 The children came down with chickenpox ☐

a I always pick up a virus from other people in the waiting room.

b and had to be kept at home until their spots healed.

c and spent all night throwing up.

d I don't think he could fight off a common cold.

e I passed out and banged my head really badly.

f it was very inflamed and I was in agony.

Grammar

A Circle the correct words.

1 It was Jess **herself / himself** who decided it was best if she ate more vegetables.
2 **Those / Them** who don't approve of the decision should write to or email the director.
3 Unfortunately, there's **anything / nothing** the doctor can do to help him.
4 My grandparents have given **each other / another** a lot of happiness over the years.
5 **Anyone / All** who'd like to come to the gathering is very welcome.
6 I think their relationship is quite serious as they've already met **one other's / one another's** parents.
7 I don't know if I should buy **these / those** shoes here or **these / those** over there.
8 I'm afraid **every / all** of these medicines are now out of date. You mustn't use them.

B Complete the text with these words.

> everyone   herself   nothing   others   some   someone   something   yourself

Art therapy

After her cancer diagnosis, Celia and her husband were devastated when they realised this wasn't **(1)** _____ that was going to go away in a few weeks or months. But then Celia decided she had to pull **(2)** _____ together and be positive to give her recovery a chance. So when one of the nurses at the hospital suggested art therapy, she jumped at the chance. Even though she had never painted before, she loved going to the sessions from the start. '**(3)** _____ is incredibly supportive. **(4)** _____ of the patients were brilliant artists and just came for the company. **(5)** _____, like me, had hardly picked up a paintbrush and really appreciated the help they got. It's brilliant because you forget **(6)** _____ and what is happening to your body.' And now, two years later, Celia is much better. '**(7)** _____ is certain, I know, but I'm enjoying each day as it comes. Next week, I'm exhibiting three of my paintings in the town hall and, who knows, **(8)** _____ may even buy one!'

C Underline one adverb or adverb phrase in each sentence.

1 My brother never goes to the gym because he's lazy.
2 Alice is going to stay with her aunt and uncle.
3 I'll hand my homework in tomorrow.
4 Thomas is leaving in three weeks.
5 I've taken some painkillers to get rid of my headache.
6 These instructions are incredibly complicated.

D Find and correct the mistakes in the sentences.

1 I will only go if it is absolute necessary. _____
2 Oh, no! The car alarm has gone off and the baby is widely awake. _____
3 You have to work extremely hardly if you want to get into medical school. _____
4 These shoes are really uncomfortable small. I should have got a bigger pair. _____
5 This is a high effective weight loss programme. It's well worth following. _____
6 Unfortunate, many patients wait more than an hour before they are seen by the doctor. _____
7 Strange enough, even though it was boring, I'd go to a cricket match again. _____
8 It's so annoying! She always arrives lately or early. Why can't she just be on time? _____

E Complete the sentences with the correct form of the words.

1 I'm going to stop reading this book. It's _____ boring.   **DESPERATE**

2 Henry has been very tired of _____. We're not sure what's wrong with him.   **LATE**

3 Charles is very ambitious. He has always aimed _____, no matter what he's doing.   **HIGH**

4 Gran always unwrapped presents _____ so she could reuse the paper.   **CAREFUL**

5 Frank was _____ devastated when he heard the terrible news.   **UTTER**

6 That ring is May's most _____ prized possession. Her mother gave it to her.   **HIGH**

7 Please don't drive so _____ on this road. It's really dangerous.   **FAST**

8 Paul has been feeling much better _____. He'll be back at work very soon.   **LATE**

Listening

You will hear a radio interview about flu pandemics. For questions 1–6, choose the best answer, a, b, c or d.

1 How does Andrew define what he does for a living?
   a He looks for cures for infectious diseases.
   b He educates people on personal hygiene.
   c He studies the origin, spread and prevention of diseases in populations.
   d He looks for ways to prevent conditions like obesity and heart disease.

2 Many healthy pigs were killed in 2009 because
   a they caused the swine flu pandemic.
   b infected pigs had passed the virus on to humans.
   c eating pork from pigs with flu could transmit the disease.
   d it was thought the swine flu pandemic had originated from infected pigs.

3 What do experts know about the origin of the 2009 flu epidemic?
   a They have no idea where it originated.
   b They know the first diagnosis was in Mexico.
   c Experts are sure it originated outside Mexico.
   d The first boy to be diagnosed lived in Mexico City.

4 How many people died from the H1N1 virus in the 2009 pandemic?
   a fewer than 18,500
   b over 600,000
   c close to 20,000
   d in excess of 300,000

5 Most researchers believe that the Spanish flu pandemic resulted in
   a a minimum of 25,000,000 deaths.
   b fewer than 25,000,000 deaths.
   c fewer deaths than those caused by World War I.
   d over 100,000,000 deaths.

6 Today, flu epidemics are likely to cause fewer deaths than they used to because
   a there is a cure.
   b everybody is vaccinated.
   c people know how to prevent contagion.
   d people wash their hands more.

Writing

A Read the writing task below and write T (true) or F (false).

> *You work for an adventure travel company. You have been asked to produce an information sheet giving trekkers advice on a three-day excursion in the jungle, based on the following areas:*
> - *clothes*
> - *equipment*
> - *sleeping arrangements*
> - *health and safety*

Write your information sheet.

1 You are writing the information for your colleagues. ☐

2 You should write in an informal, friendly style. ☐

3 You will need to explain what trekkers should bring. ☐

4 You shouldn't mention any of the risks involved in jungle trekking. ☐

B Read the model information sheet and complete it with these headings.

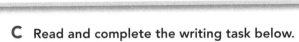

A great night's sleep   Comfortable clothes   Health and safety   Essential stuff

Jungle tour

Here are some tips to ensure you have a brilliant and safe jungle adventure.

(1) _____

With daytime temperatures up to 32°C and humidity levels close to 80%, it will feel very hot and sticky. There will also be plenty of mosquitoes. Follow these guidelines for a comfortable trek:

- Wear cotton clothing and bring a spare set of clothes and extra socks.
- Wear long trousers and long-sleeved tops to protect your skin from sunburn and insects.
- Wear a hat, walking boots and long socks.

(2) _____

You'll be amazed how noisy the jungle is after dark. If you think this will keep you awake, bring earplugs with you.

(3) _____

The jungle is rainy and full of wildlife. Here are the essentials to keep you safe and comfortable:

- Make sure your backpack is waterproof.
- Bring a top quality mosquito net with you.
- Spray insect repellent at least twice a day.
- Never, ever go barefoot in the jungle!

(4) _____

It's a good idea to pack a few basics in a first-aid kit.

- plasters for those inevitable blisters
- insect repellent and suncream

Follow these tips and you'll have a fantastic time!

C Read and complete the writing task below.

> *You work for a sports and adventure summer camp. You have been asked to produce an information sheet giving campers advice on the following areas:*
> - *available sports and activities*
> - *clothes and equipment*
> - *sleeping arrangements*
> - *health and safety*

*Write your **information sheet** in 220–260 words in an appropriate style.*

Watch the clock!

 Spend 5 minutes reading the task and planning your information sheet.

 Spend 30 minutes writing your information sheet.

 Spend 5 minutes checking and editing your information sheet.

Remember!

The main aim of an information sheet is to communicate facts clearly and concisely. Use headings and bullet points to organise your facts, but make sure you have an appropriate introduction and conclusion. Use a suitable register: formal, semi-formal or informal, depending on your audience. See the Writing Reference for information sheets on page 177 of the Student's Book for further help.

4 Lights, Camera, Action!

Reading

Read the text and choose the answer (a, b, c or d) which best fits according to the text.

Hollywood takes on Bollywood

As well as being the wealthiest and most populous city in India, with over 20 million inhabitants, Mumbai (formerly Bombay) is home to India's incredibly prolific Hindi-language film industry. This is no cottage industry. Every year, Bollywood – the word is a portmanteau of **B**ombay and **Hollywood** – produces roughly twice the number of feature films that are made in Hollywood. Those Hindi films are watched by an audience of 3 billion people worldwide, whereas the total audience for Hollywood films is only about 2.6 billion. However, the surprising truth behind those statistics is that 80% of the revenue from Bollywood films comes from inside India, while 50% of the money made from Hollywood films comes from outside the US, but almost none of it from India.

Anyone who has watched both a traditional Bollywood film and a Hollywood blockbuster will perhaps understand why there is so little crossover between the audiences for these films. They are simply worlds apart. From the perspective of an audience used to watching Hollywood blockbusters, Bollywood films are puzzling and impossible to categorise. They follow conventions that are simply not reflected in American films. Bollywood films are always very long (three hours is normal) and therefore they have an intermission. They often combine elements of what a western audience would consider different genres within the same film. For example, whatever the storyline and wherever it takes place, a Bollywood film will almost invariably contain scenes with singing and dancing. Those scenes will involve lots of extras in costume and often be filmed in the Swiss Alps, even though the main story probably takes place in an Indian city.

To the western eye, the transition between these scenes is abrupt and startling. To the Indian, no film is complete without good songs and dances. In other words, having a seamless plot is considered less important than making a strong visual and aural impact.

Hollywood would love nothing more than to break into the vast and potentially lucrative Indian market, but their efforts have been in vain. Indian audiences just don't like American films. Now, having failed to sell their own films into India, most of the big Hollywood studios are investing in Bollywood-style films. These are shot in India in Hindi, using Indian actors, directors and crews. However, so far these, too, have enjoyed little success. This is perhaps less to do with cultural issues in the films themselves (after all they are, except for the funding, entirely Indian) than with issues relating to the Indian marketplace. The truth is that most Bollywood films don't make money either. In fact, Indian studios only succeed by producing many films and hoping that one or two of them become hits. Up until now, Hollywood has only dipped its toe into the water of Indian cinema. If it wants to succeed in the Indian box office, it will probably need to jump in.

In the meantime, Hollywood and Bollywood will remain poles apart. As one Indian reviewer said of the serious Hollywood epic *Ghandi* about the life of Indian civil rights activist, Mahatma Ghandi, 'I thought the film was pretty good, actually, but it perhaps lacked a few song and dance numbers.'

1 Bollywood films are
   a twice as popular as Hollywood films.
   b mainly watched by Indians in India.
   c as popular outside their country of origin as Hollywood films.
   d produced in small-scale industries.

2 How much of Hollywood's revenue comes from non-American audiences?
   a a fifth
   b less than a fifth
   c half
   d more than a half

3 Compared to Bollywood films, Hollywood films
   a are unstructured and tend to have weak story lines.
   b could be considered plain and unadorned.
   c usually straddle different styles.
   d may appear unrealistic and surprising.

4 Indian audiences prefer the films they watch to
   a have an unambiguous and succinct plot.
   b be lengthy and include features of musicals.
   c be set in Switzerland.
   d be stronger visually than musically.

5 The author of the article believes that Hollywood
   a needs to invest heavily in Indian films.
   b has no options but to invest in Bollywood films.
   c has already achieved success in Bollywood.
   d must introduce Bollywood-style films to a worldwide audience.

6 As a business model, Indian producers
   a make few, carefully-researched, high-quality films which are often financially successful.
   b make musicals inspired by Hollywood, which are watched all over the world.
   c are mainly concerned in producing art rather than making money.
   d rely on a few films to be box office successes and make money for the industry.

Vocabulary

A Circle the correct words.

1 This is a traditional play – you would never call it groundbreaking / heart-warming.
2 I saw the most heart-rending / cutting-edge film last night – even my father had a tear in his eye!
3 My producer / agent is always putting my name forward for films and TV shows. I'm never out of work.
4 Diana is an extraordinary film editor / boom operator. When she puts a film together, she makes magic.
5 We have to listen to the director / producer. After all, without him, there would be no financing for this film.
6 That actress could never learn her acts / lines and always had someone holding them up for her in the studio.
7 I'm a(n) usher / gaffer at the National Theatre, so I can stand at the back and watch all the plays for free.
8 James's ambition is to put on set / stage plays. He just loves the theatre.

B Complete the text with these words.

> act   aisles   backstage   foyer   intermission   row   show   usher

Birthday surprise

I had a fantastic time on my 21st birthday last Friday. Knowing how much I love the theatre, my parents had got tickets to a Broadway **(1)** _____, the musical *Mamma Mia*. I was so excited. But you can't imagine how thrilled I was when we walked into the theatre and there was my best friend, Sophie, waiting for us in the **(2)** _____. She'd come all the way from Paris! But that wasn't all. When it was time to go in and the **(3)** _____ showed us to our seats, I couldn't believe we were in the fifth **(4)** _____ from the front! My parents couldn't have got better seats. We had champagne during the **(5)** _____, after the first **(6)** _____, and by the end of the play we were dancing in the **(7)** _____. But that wasn't all, before going out to dinner, we were allowed **(8)** _____ to meet some of the actors. My uncle had arranged it, as he knows the director. All I can is it was the best night of my life!

STAGE DOOR

C Choose the correct answers.

1 The director was delighted, as the rehearsal had gone ___ a hitch.
  a in   b with   c without

2 Paul is an architect ___ profession, but he's been working as a set designer for the last couple of years.
  a for   b by   c on

3 I'm not really interested in a career ___ showbiz. It's too precarious.
  a in   b on   c at

4 Thomas is playing the tyrannical king in his school play and when he gets home after a performance, he's so bossy it's as if he's still ___ character.
  a with   b in   c for

5 The band arrived ___ the accompaniment of wild cheering from the crowd.
  a to   b at   c by

6 She's not the sort of person to put herself forward. She prefers to be ___ the background.
  a behind   b in   c for

7 Susan is prepared to drop everything ___ a moment's notice just to hear her favourite band.
  a without   b by   c at

8 At the film studio, we were allowed ___ the set of one of the TV shows we often watched at home.
  a in   b at   c on

D The words in bold are in the wrong sentences. Write each word next to the correct sentence.

1 Even though he's been in a lot of films, I think Al Pacino gave his best **portrayal** ever in *The Godfather II*. _____

2 *Rango* won the Academy Award for Best **Lead** Feature at the 2012 Oscars. It's all about a pet chameleon and it's good fun, but still not as good as the cartoons of my childhood. _____

3 Daniel Radcliffe played the **role** in all the *Harry Potter* films. I think he was brilliant. _____

4 Last year, Emily had a small **ovation** in the school play. This year, she's one of the leads. _____

5 If you decide you'd like to be involved in the play, you have to commit to coming to **performance** twice a week until opening night. _____

6 His **rehearsals** of Othello in Shakespeare's play was second to none. _____

7 Oscar used to suffer terribly from stage **animated**, but now he has learnt to relax and control his breathing, and has much less trouble going on stage. _____

8 Their performance is so remarkable that they've had a standing **fright** every night since the play was first performed. _____

E Match the first parts of the sentences 1–8 to the second parts a–h.

1 We saw a brilliant film last night that really tugged ☐

2 I don't want to see another chick flick! Why ☐

3 Simon has the biggest dressing room ☐

4 The most important film festivals are probably ☐

5 The studio always makes sure it releases four or five ☐

6 I think *The Hobbit* is the sort of film ☐

7 Let's go and see a comedy. I can't ☐

8 Going to the opening night was brilliant. We saw ☐

a Berlin, Cannes and Venice, also known as the big three.

b bear another tale of woe.

c don't we go to the new James Bond film?

d all the stars on the red carpet.

e at the heartstrings. There wasn't a dry eye in the house.

f children's films in time for the summer holidays.

g because he's the star of the show.

h that appeals to adults as well as children.

Grammar

A Complete the sentences with the correct form of the verbs in brackets.

1 I still haven't forgiven the director for _____ Tony the lead in the play. (not give)

2 I can't afford _____ opera tickets these days. They're too expensive. (buy)

3 _____ is a wonderful profession, but it's quite precarious. (act)

4 You'd better _____ or you'll miss the beginning of the film. (hurry)

5 Audience members aren't allowed _____ backstage at the theatre. (go)

6 I remember _____ *The Sound of Music* when I was a child. I loved it! (watch)

7 Don't tell me you forgot _____ the tickets! I reminded you at least twice. (bring)

8 When my manager persuaded the director _____ me audition again, I got the part. (let)

B Find and correct the mistakes in the sentences.

1 We're really looking forward to see his latest film. _____
2 Do you feel like to watch a film tonight? _____
3 Henry enjoys to go to the theatre but not to the cinema. _____
4 Would you prefer see a romantic comedy or an adventure film? _____
5 The director made her to do the scene again and again until she got it right. _____
6 Anita is too tired playing her violin for you tonight. _____
7 I can't imagine never be able to go out without being recognised. _____
8 She was always late for rehearsals and risked to lose her part. _____

C Choose the correct answers.

1 Oliver persuaded his brother ___ him his laptop computer.
   a to lend   b lend   c lending

2 I don't think he's going to forgive me for ___ his mobile phone.
   a to lose   b lose   c losing

3 On second thoughts, you might ___ this film as much as I thought you would.
   a not to enjoy   b not enjoy   c not enjoying

4 Have you been ___ yet this winter?
   a to ski   b ski   c skiing

5 It's no good ___ about the weather. There's nothing you can do about it.
   a to worry   b worry   c worrying

6 I can remember ___ all afternoon at the cinema when I was growing up.
   a to spend   b spending   c spend

7 I can't persuade Daniel ___ any more time practising.
   a to spend   b spend   c spending

8 Although Beatrice was prepared ___ the soundtrack, she actually loved it.
   a not to like   b not like   c not liking

D Circle the correct words in the dialogue.

The movie

Lucy   Hi, Marina. I've just been to the cinema.

Marina   Oh, what did you see?

Lucy   Well, I thought we were going to see a romantic comedy, but **(1)** in fact / by the way we saw an action movie.

Marina   Really? I'm surprised. I seem to remember you're not too keen on that kind of film.

Lucy   You're right. **(2)** Apparently / As a matter of fact, I hate action movies!

Marina   So what happened?

Lucy   Well, Justin bought the tickets, but **(3)** evidently / by all means, it was Alex's fault.

Marina   Alex's fault? Why?

Lucy   Well, **(4)** after all / apparently Alex told Justin that *Destroyer III* was a chick flick and that I would love it.

Marina   No!

Lucy   I know. Well, **(5)** obviously / still, Alex was joking.

Marina   But Justin must have told you the title of the film.

Lucy   He did but, **(6)** surely / quite honestly, I don't think I was really listening. That's what's so annoying!

Marina   **(7)** Anyway / I mean, I suppose Justin loved it!

Lucy   Funnily enough, he didn't, really.

4 Lights, Camera, Action!

E Match the sentences 1–6 to the sentences a–f.

1 There's always someone the director blames when a scene goes wrong. ☐
2 There's no point leaving now after waiting in the rain for three hours. ☐
3 We took my niece to the ballet last night. ☐
4 George told off everyone at the audition. ☐
5 I didn't enjoy the play at all. ☐
6 It's an enjoyable film, I suppose, but it's nothing special. ☐

a Admittedly, they were all messing about and deserved it.
b Naturally, as a budding ballerina, she adored every minute.
c Namely me!
d Quite frankly, it was so awful, I wish I'd stayed at home.
e In other words, I don't think it'll be a major hit.
f After all, we won't get another chance to see him in the flesh.

Listening

You will hear five people talking about their roles in film, cinema and TV. Complete both tasks as you listen.

Task 1 For questions 1–5, choose from the list A–H the person who is speaking.

1 Speaker 1 ☐
2 Speaker 2 ☐
3 Speaker 3 ☐
4 Speaker 4 ☐
5 Speaker 5 ☐

A a special-effects makeup artist
B a set designer
C a costume designer
D a theatre director
E a successful TV actor
F a film actor
G a doorman at a hotel
H a sound engineer

Task 2 For questions 6–10, choose from the list A–H what each person is expressing.

6 Speaker 1 ☐
7 Speaker 2 ☐
8 Speaker 3 ☐
9 Speaker 4 ☐
10 Speaker 5 ☐

A dissatisfaction with a recent job
B joy at returning to his/her past career
C amazement at getting a wonderful job
D irritation due to working so long
E delight at his/her fame
F annoyance at working with difficult people
G disappointment at not being recognised
H acceptance of a current situation

Writing

A Read the writing task below and answer the questions.

You see the following announcement on a theatre review website.

> *Have you been to any outstanding plays or musicals recently? If so, why not write a review about it and say why you would recommend it.*
>
> The best review will be published in our next issue.

1 Who will be reading your review?
2 What will you be writing about?
3 Can you write about films or TV?
4 Can you choose a play you didn't like?

B Read the model review and complete it with these words and phrases.

a All in all
b brilliantly adapted for the theatre
c But the real stroke of genius

d unreservedly and wholeheartedly
e made the whole experience unforgettable
f to appeal to modern audiences

Matilda the Musical

Time Out magazine called it 'the best British musical in years', and other reviewers were equally generous in their praise. Appealing to children, parents and grandparents alike, it was bound to be a smash hit.

With reviews like these, I was determined to see *Matilda the Musical* when I came to London and I'm delighted to say I wasn't disappointed. Roald Dahl's children's book has been **(1)** _____ by writer Denis Kelly and Australian comedian, composer and songwriter Tim Minchin. Although it remains true to the spirit of the original novel, it has been brought up to date **(2)** _____. There are many hilarious touches, like the ballroom dancing scene between Matilda's mother and her slimy dance partner, who perform a Latin dance worthy of *Strictly Come Dancing*, one of Britain's favourite TV shows.

However, what **(3)** _____ were the brilliant songs, catchy and hilarious, and the extraordinarily clever lyrics. Added to that were the marvellous and inventive set, the dazzling choreography and the extraordinarily talented cast. **(4)** _____ must be casting a male actor as Miss Trunchbull, the wonderfully evil Olympic hammer-throwing headmistress at Matilda's school. He very nearly steals the show and I don't doubt he will go down in theatre history as one of the great villains of the stage.

(5) _____, it was a hugely entertaining evening and I'm still humming the songs now, two weeks later. So, finally, let me recommend *Matilda the Musical* **(6)** _____. If you get the chance to go, don't miss it!

C Read and complete the writing task below.

> *A website you visit features film and theatre reviews written by its readers. You decide to contribute to the website. Write a review of a film or play you have seen, explaining why you did or did not enjoy it and whether or not you would recommend it to others.*

*Write your **review** in 220–260 words in an appropriate style.*

Watch the clock!

 Spend 5 minutes reading the task and planning your review.

 Spend 30 minutes writing your review.

 Spend 5 minutes checking and editing your review.

Remember!

When writing a review your main aim is to describe what you have seen without giving away the whole plot. Be clear about the genre of the piece and the audience it is aimed for. Describe the acting, direction, set and costume design, for example. Finally, give your opinion and decide whether you would recommend it or not. See the Writing Reference for reviews on page 178 of the Student's Book for further help.

Vocabulary

A Choose the correct answers.

1 Ian fell asleep ___ to the noise around him.
   a unconscious
   b ignorant
   c oblivious
   d insensible

2 I was given ___ instructions to follow.
   a precise
   b defined
   c vast
   d vivid

3 The doctor ___ antibiotics for my chest infection.
   a monitored
   b responded
   c arranged
   d prescribed

4 It's easy to suffer from ___ in this heat.
   a drying
   b parching
   c dehydration
   d hydration

5 The baby couldn't drink and had to receive fluids ___.
   a inwardly
   b intravenously
   c infectiously
   d internally

6 There is no ___ vaccination yet for malaria.
   a effective
   b efficient
   c beneficial
   d functional

7 Luke is at home today because he's ___ a cold.
   a come up with
   b come away with
   c come down with
   d come far with

8 This purple mark on my arm is just a(n) ___.
   a sore
   b wound
   c bruise
   d injury

9 The largest internal ___ is the liver.
   a piece
   b structure
   c part
   d organ

10 She's very ill, but we don't think it's ___.
   a closing
   b terminal
   c ending
   d terminating

11 It's a ___ story about love and friendship.
   a heart-moving
   b heart-warming
   c heart-cheering
   d heart-soothing

12 It's a very long play, but there are two ___.
   a intermissions
   b interludes
   c breaks
   d pauses

13 Don't sit in the front ___. It's too close to the screen.
   a line
   b file
   c row
   d aisle

14 The concert was bad because we hadn't ___ enough.
   a reviewed
   b coached
   c assembled
   d rehearsed

15 We were invited ___ to meet the actors.
   a offstage
   b on stage
   c backstage
   d behind stage

16 Her best ___ was as the nurse in *Romeo and Juliet*.
   a show
   b character
   c performance
   d appearance

17 It was wonderful! The ceremony went ___ a hitch.
   a with
   b without
   c in
   d within

18 Who was the female ___ in *Titanic*?
   a lead
   b leader
   c principal
   d prime

19 His film ___ of President Lincoln was amazing.
   a representation
   b interpretation
   c portrait
   d portrayal

20 That actor suffers from terrible ___ fright.
   a platform
   b theatre
   c dramatic
   d stage

Grammar

B **Choose the correct answers.**

1 Look over there! ___ the one I was telling you about.
   a This is
   b That's
   c These are
   d Those are

2 Have you met? Let me introduce you. ___ Tanya.
   a Here is
   b There is
   c This is
   d That is

3 You sound worried. Is ___ OK?
   a anything
   b something
   c anybody
   d everything

4 I loved it! ___ novels are as brilliant as this one.
   a Few
   b Any
   c Each
   d Either

5 They admired ___ dresses.
   a each other
   b each other's
   c another's
   d one another

6 Miriam offered to help ___. She's a good friend.
   a no hesitation
   b in hesitation
   c without hesitation
   d hesitating

7 It's ___ hot today.
   a uncomfortable
   b not comfortable
   c comfortless
   d uncomfortably

8 I was so tired I could ___ keep my eyes open.
   a hard
   b hardly
   c absolute
   d absolutely

9 You know you haven't worked ___ enough.
   a hard
   b hardly
   c high
   d highly

10 Although they are ___ rich, they live in a modest house.
   a incredible
   b widely
   c enormous
   d enormously

11 You really should avoid ___ up so late.
   a stay
   b to stay
   c staying
   d have stayed

12 Did you know ___ was his passion?
   a sail
   b to sail
   c go sailing
   d sailing

13 Nadia was too scared ___ that horror movie.
   a watch
   b to watch
   c watching
   d have watched

14 They weren't strong enough ___.
   a to lift it
   b lifting it
   c lifting
   d for lift

15 You'll ___ to your destination by bus.
   a taken
   b taking
   c be taken
   d be taking

16 I'm afraid I forgot ___ milk. I'll go out and get some now.
   a buy
   b to buy
   c buying
   d to have bought

17 I can't remember ___ your wallet. Sorry!
   a see
   b to see
   c seeing
   d have seen

18 She was hoping ___ for the lead part in the school play.
   a choose
   b choosing
   c to choose
   d to be chosen

19 I can't say I enjoyed it. ___, it was my own fault. I didn't make much of an effort.
   a By the way
   b Surely
   c Still
   d Admittedly

20 You choose the film. ___, it's your birthday.
   a As a matter of fact
   b After all
   c Obviously
   d Naturally

33

Review 2

Use of English

C Choose the correct answers.

Sleep study

A new study shows that a lack of sleep can make vaccines less **(1)** ___. The study was conducted on 125 participants in which researchers **(2)** ___ their sleep patterns after being given the vaccine used for **(3)** ___ off hepatitis B. The **(4)** ___ was administered according to a **(5)** ___ set of procedures. The first and second doses were given one month apart from each other, and the final one was given after six months. At that point, the participants were tested for proteins in their bodies that normally **(6)** ___ to the presence of hepatitis B. Surprisingly, there were **(7)** ___ differences between the two groups: the participants who slept less than 6.5 hours per night on average had a significantly lower amount of these proteins than people who slept more than 7 hours per night. The group lacking in sleep were more than 11 times as likely to **(8)** ___ down with hepatitis B. Research has already proven that a lack of sleep can **(9)** ___ people's ability to ward off colds, the **(10)** ___ and other types of illnesses. This specific study shows that a lack of sleep may affect the body's immune system, which naturally helps the body to **(11)** ___ from illnesses. It seems that sleep may have its own **(12)** ___ properties.

1	a	valuable	b	successful	c	effective	d	qualified
2	a	practised	b	prescribed	c	consulted	d	monitored
3	a	fighting	b	passing	c	picking	d	throwing
4	a	function	b	property	c	discovery	d	treatment
5	a	contended	b	wholesome	c	physical	d	precise
6	a	consult	b	respond	c	relieve	d	sprain
7	a	vivid	b	vast	c	oblivious	d	scatty
8	a	arrive	b	get	c	come	d	go
9	a	harm	b	wound	c	injure	d	heal
10	a	disease	b	flu	c	sickness	d	condition
11	a	suffer	b	provide	c	recover	d	result
12	a	medicinal	b	medical	c	medicated	d	medicine

D Complete the text with the correct form of the words.

The hypothalamus

The hypothalamus is a part of the brain that controls **(1)** _____ functions such as hunger, sleep, and body temperature. It tells us when there is an **(2)** _____ in our bodies, for instance, it indicates that we're becoming **(3)** _____ by making us feel **(4)** _____ when we don't drink enough water. It is located in the centre of our brains and is about the size of an almond. The hypothalamus works with the body's nervous system and **(5)** _____ organs to interpret signals that come from all areas of the body. It has a way of telling us when we're **(6)** _____ that we need to change our diets. The hypothalamus also controls behavioural responses to emotions. It explains why, for example, an actor who has stage **(7)** _____ can't go out on stage, or why when we see sad films that pull on our **(8)** _____, we tend to cry. Poor nutrition can cause the hypothalamus to suffer from **(9)** _____ and if left unchecked, these problems can lead to changes in weight, fatigue, **(10)** _____, and hair loss.

BODY
BALANCE
HYDRATE
THIRST

INSIDE
NOURISH

FRIGHTEN
HEART
ORDER
HEAD

E Think of one word only that can be used appropriately in all three sentences.

1 The play is considered a tragedy, but there's some humour _____ in for laughs.

I'm sorry I left you waiting at the theatre – I must have gotten the dates _____ up.

I'm not sure if I liked the play or not, so I'm having _____ feelings about it.

2 You're promising to buy the tickets, but _____ is cheap – I want to see the tickets first.

Although her mother tried to _____ her out of it, Sheila moved to London to act in theatre.

You're an actor in film and I'm an actor on stage – I'm afraid we don't _____ the same language.

3 His brother was working in film, so Jed decided to follow his _____ and work in film also.

If you think you can do your job better than me, then by all means – _____ the way!

Jeffrey won't be playing the male _____ in the film; they chose another actor.

4 The play will be shut down until further _____.

The director failed to take _____ of the extra set pieces on stage.

If the star of the play doesn't show, let me know and I'll be there at a moment's _____.

5 You need to grow up and become serious about your future. Don't _____ the fool.

I'm not sure what we should do tonight – let's just _____ it by ear.

Whether I'm at work or at _____, I try to enjoy myself.

F Complete the second sentences so that they have a similar meaning to the first sentences using the words in bold. Use between three and six words.

1 Joseph has been acting since he graduated from drama school.

PROFESSION

Joseph has been _____ since graduating from drama school.

2 Don't believe her story – not a word of it is true.

ACT

Don't believe what she's telling you – she's _____.

3 Michael continued to talk like a pirate backstage even though his role had finished.

CHARACTER

Even though his role had finished, Michael _____ backstage.

4 Helen let nothing stand in her way of becoming a film star.

OBSTACLES

Helen _____ in order to become a film star.

5 She changed her mind and decided not to attend the play.

HEART

She decided not to attend the play because she _____.

6 He wasn't sure the audience at the back could hear, so he yelled loudly.

LUNGS

He shouted _____ so the audience at the back could hear.

7 The two stars of the film hate each other and argue all the time.

THROATS

The two stars of the film don't get on and are _____.

8 You may not like what I have to say, but you don't have to yell at me.

BITE

You don't have to _____ if you don't like what I'm saying.

Reading

Read the texts and choose the answer (a, b, c or d) which fits best according to the text.

FITNESS OR FATNESS

With obesity rates in most industrialised countries at record levels and more and more of us leading sedentary lives, it is hardly surprising that there is so much obsession in the media about the importance of curbing our calorie intake and increasing the amount of exercise we take. The United Kingdom Department of Health recommends a daily calorie intake for men of just over 2,500 and for women of just below 2,000. However, there is a small group of people whose goal is to consume up to twice this number of calories in an attempt to attain peak physical fitness. These are the professional athletes.

Olympic swimmers train long and hard. On top of ten gruelling sessions in the pool, they do strength training in the gym and undergo physiotherapy. Needless to say, they burn a lot of calories. During the 2008 Beijing Olympics, Michael Phelps allegedly told the American broadcaster NBC that he consumed up to 12,000 calories a day while training. He has since claimed that this was a myth. However, Olympic athletes certainly need a huge amount of fuel to be able to train at such intensity.

But it's not just about calories. It's important to fuel up from the right food groups at the right time. While training, athletes require carbohydrates to keep their energy levels high and protein to repair and build muscle. They also need essential vitamins and minerals, which they get from fresh fruit and vegetables. These foods also supply them with healthy fats. Keeping hydrated is equally important. Athletes lose a lot of water through sweat.

The day before a competition, long-distance runners and swimmers do what is known as 'carb-loading'. That is to say, they eat lots of carbohydrates that the muscles will store as energy to be released during the event the following day. Of course, athletes face the same problem that the rest of us do. If they eat more calories than they burn, they will put on weight. Being an Olympic athlete cannot be a piece of cake.

FOOD INTOLERANCE OR FOOD ALLERGY?

We are all likely at some point in our lives to have a bad reaction to a certain food. In many cases, it may be as a result of food poisoning, which is not a reaction to the food itself, but to contaminants in the food as a result of poor storage, handling or cooking. In far fewer cases, it may mean that we have a food intolerance or a food allergy. But what is the difference and why is the distinction important?

A food intolerance is often caused by a difficulty in digesting a particular substance (such as lactose, a sugar present in milk). There may be digestive symptoms such as stomach cramps or nausea, but these are usually triggered only after large amounts of the substance are consumed and the symptoms usually occur several hours after the food has been eaten. People with an intolerance to a certain food, learn to avoid it but may eat small amounts without experiencing symptoms.

A food allergy, on the other hand, is an abnormal response to a food caused by a reaction in the immune system to a particular protein. While symptoms are usually mild and may be similar to those produced by a food intolerance, they are much more varied and may in rare cases be life threatening. These include itching in the mouth or throat, swelling of the face, lips and tongue, asthma, and – much more rarely – a sudden drop in blood pressure (known as anaphylaxis). People with strong allergies to food must avoid those foods at all costs.

The foods that most commonly trigger allergic reactions are milk, eggs, nuts and shellfish. The good news is that food allergies affect only about 6% of children and 3% of adults. The lower figure in adults is because some of the allergies more common in children, such as an allergy to milk or to eggs, resolve themselves over time while allergies to nuts and shellfish tend to last a lifetime.

LACTOSE FR

1 What is the main cause of obesity in women?
   a consuming more food than they burn
   b consuming too many carbohydrates
   c not eating a balanced diet
   d not training hard enough

2 The day before competing, athletes
   a eat as much as 12,000 calories.
   b eat carbohydrates, proteins and vitamins.
   c fill up with carbohydrates as fuel for the body.
   d consume more calories than they will burn.

3 What is the main cause of food poisoning?
   a an allergy or intolerance to certain foods
   b food which contains harmful bacteria
   c food with substances like lactose
   d food that is handled too much

4 How is an allergy different to an intolerance?
   a A food intolerance can be fatal.
   b Only allergies cause pain.
   c Allergy symptoms take longer to appear.
   d An allergy can cause serious symptoms.

Vocabulary

A Complete the words in the sentences.

1 Daniel isn't feeling well and has lost his a _ _ _ _ _ _ _.

2 You mustn't have sweet fizzy drinks to q _ _ _ _ _ your thirst.

3 What an amazing meal! It was a c _ _ _ _ _ _ _ triumph.

4 What's your favourite ethnic c _ _ _ _ _ _? Mine's Indian. I just love curries.

5 'Go on, have another biscuit.' 'OK, just one. I can't r _ _ _ _ _ these delicious chocolate ones.'

6 Don't eat so much junk food or you will p _ _ _ on the pounds and become obese.

7 Make sure you s _ _ _ _ _ the casserole really slowly. You mustn't let it boil or you'll ruin it.

8 Lucy decided she needed to s _ _ _ a few pounds before going on holiday, so she went on a strict diet.

B Decide if these words are related to how food tastes, to the cooking of food or to ways of eating. Write T (taste), C (cooking) or E (eating) next to the words.

1 munch ☐
2 poach ☐
3 gobble ☐
4 bland ☐

5 sour ☐
6 bake ☐
7 bitter ☐
8 blanch ☐

C Circle the correct words.

1 The Queen welcomed the President to the United Kingdom with a spread / banquet at Buckingham Palace.

2 Can I have a second platter / helping, please? I'm still really hungry.

3 We were ravenous / stunted after fasting for two days, so everything tasted delicious.

4 Oh, no, look! The bread has gone mouldy / fizzy. There are green bits all over it. You can't eat it!

5 This cake is absolutely scrumptious / appetising! Can I have the recipe?

6 The drought went on for months, nothing grew in the fields and the animals famished / starved to death.

7 Snacks like crisps and roasted nuts are too salty / acidic for young children. They shouldn't eat them.

8 Can I have a little nibble / sip of your drink? It looks so delicious.

D Choose the correct answers.

1 There's a casserole in the fridge that you can have for dinner. All you have to do is ___ it up.
   a blanch   **b** brew   **c** warm

2 Paul ___ up an amazing meal for ten people in a couple of hours. I don't know how he did it!
   a beat   **b** whipped   **c** packed

3 'How's your aunt?' 'She's full of ___ and very cheerful. Incredible when you think she's 84!'
   a peas   **b** beans   **c** cake

4 What's wrong? You didn't have a first course and now you're just ___ at your main course.
   a picking   **b** dining   **c** tucking

5 My mum loves this stuff. She thinks it's the best thing since ___ bread!
   a chopped   **b** cracked   **c** sliced

6 You know, you will just have to compromise. You can't always have your ___ and eat it.
   a pie   **b** cake   **c** cream

7 When he was training, Lucas could ___ away half a chicken and a pizza in one sitting.
   a pack   **b** dine   **c** polish

8 We've got a delicious chicken pie for lunch today. I can't wait to ___ in.
   a dine   **b** tuck   **c** pack

Grammar

A Complete the second sentences so that they have a similar meaning to the first sentences using the words in bold.

1 George and Sophie had dinner in a restaurant because they didn't feel like cooking.
   OUT
   George and Sophie _____ because they didn't feel like cooking.

2 Poor Lucinda was so hungry she almost fainted, didn't she?
   OUT
   Poor Lucinda was so hungry she almost _____, didn't she?

3 You shouldn't drink your juice so fast as it's very rude.
   DOWN
   You shouldn't _____ as it's very rude.

4 I'm afraid Robert has got the flu and will have to stay in bed.
   DOWN
   I'm afraid Robert _____ and will have to stay in bed.

5 We found the house of our dreams, but the sale was cancelled.
   THROUGH
   We found the house of our dreams, but _____.

6 I'm sure Dalia will be very successful in her career because she is very ambitious.
   AHEAD
   I'm sure Dalia _____ because she is very ambitious.

7 Louis hardly touched his dinner as he wasn't hungry.
   AT
   Louis _____ as he wasn't hungry.

8 It was a fantastic dinner and we all ate with great enthusiasm.
   IN
   It was a fantastic dinner and we all _____.

B Complete the sentences with the phrasal verbs given and the correct pronoun.

1 I feel terrible. I've got a chest infection and I've been trying to _____ all week. (fight off)

2 You ate all the sweets and left none for me! Why did you _____? (polish off)

3 Julie works very quickly and the other chefs can't _____. (keep up with)

4 It's a wonderful sauce, but you must _____ slowly or it will go lumpy. (warm up)

5 Thomas has got a great recipe for chicken with ginger and garlic.
He _____ when he was experimenting in the kitchen one day. (come up with)

6 Jack is always rude to the customers, but he never gets into trouble. How does
he _____? (get away with)

C Complete the same-way question tags.

1 So, you've passed all your exams, _____ you? Well done!

2 Let's stay in tonight, _____ we?

3 I don't suppose you'd lend me your new dress, _____ you?

4 There's nothing to eat in the house, _____ there?

5 She'd like to become a chef, _____ she? That's surprising.

6 So it's my turn to cook, _____ it? I thought it was David's.

7 They gobbled up every last bit, _____ they? I'm amazed!

8 She could stay with you, _____ she? That's great!

D Circle the correct tag.

1 Mary would much rather eat in, she would / she wouldn't.

2 I see. You refuse to eat it, do you / don't you?

3 That's a fantastic chocolate cake, it is / that is.

4 Stella should cut down on the amount of salt she puts in her food, she should / she shouldn't.

5 You'd like an ice-cream, you would / would you? Let's go and get one now.

6 So you always wash up, do you / you do? What are those dishes doing there then?

7 These tomatoes aren't ripe, they are / they aren't.

8 I think we'd better clear up this mess now, I had / I do.

E Tick the correct sentences. Correct the sentences that are wrong.

1 I'm going to stick to a low-carb diet from now on, I'm not.

2 These biscuits are absolutely delicious, they are.

3 Max hasn't got any time to cook at the moment, he has.

4 I don't suppose I could use your espresso machine, do I?

5 There are lots of onions in the kitchen, are there? I can't find them!

6 She's determined to learn how to cook, Helen is.

7 You couldn't help us out just this once, could you?

8 I'm sure I brought the biscuits home with me, I had.

5 Eat Up!

Listening

You will hear eight short conversations. Choose the best answer, a, b or c, that means about the same thing as you hear or that is true according to what you hear.

1 a There isn't any butter.
   b The woman hid the butter so the man couldn't find it.
   c The man couldn't see the butter as it was behind the cheese.

2 a She didn't let him know she was going to be out for dinner.
   b He didn't look at his text messages.
   c Her message didn't arrive.

3 a She is going to train to become a chef at her school.
   b He thinks she should train before opening a restaurant.
   c She is going to open a restaurant while training to be a chef.

4 a Henry used to be slim, but he's put on a lot of weight recently.
   b Henry is large, but you wouldn't describe him as obese.
   c The woman thinks Henry should lose some weight.

5 a She knew that tomatoes originated in Mesoamerica.
   b He knows many foods we eat originated in the American continent.
   c She didn't realise that chocolate came from the Americas.

6 a The man has lost weight since he stopped eating takeaways.
   b The woman doesn't believe that the man hasn't been on a diet.
   c The man has been on a strict diet, avoiding fast food.

7 a The man agrees to cook a curry for the woman.
   b The woman wants a takeaway as she doesn't want to cook.
   c The man doesn't like any sort of fast food.

8 a She believes he doesn't want to eat with the family.
   b He has been eating a lot at work.
   c She doesn't really believe that he will change his ways.

Writing

A Read the writing task below and answer the questions.

> You are a member of the student social committee at an international college. The principal has asked you to write a proposal recommending a menu for a dinner for those students leaving the college at the end of the year.
>
> Read the extract from the principal's email below. Then, write your proposal.

1 Who is the target reader?
2 What register will you use?
3 How many menus will you discuss?
4 What do you need to recommend?

 email

From: principal@college.com
Sent: 12th June
Subject: Leaver's dinner menu

We need to choose a menu for our Leaver's Dinner next month. Here are some possibilities suggested by our students – could you please make a recommendation?

Chinese theme → exotic option, not familiar to all

Indian feast → lots of variety, spicy

American alternative → popular with everyone; not special

Mediterranean choice → healthy and varied

Write your proposal.

B Read the model proposal and write your own introduction and conclusion.

Proposal for Leaver's Dinner Menu

Introduction

_____

_____

Chinese theme
This is an exotic and original option. Some of our students have eaten Chinese food, especially takeaways, and would enjoy the variety of dishes. However, other students may be reluctant to try it if they've never had it before.

Indian feast
This is also an ethnic choice, which would be very popular with a great many students. The variety of meat and vegetarian dishes is appealing. On the other hand, it may be too spicy for some of our students.

American alternative
Everyone loves burgers, chips, pizza and hotdogs. Having said that, this is a rather informal choice and not really appropriate for a Leaver's Dinner. It probably wouldn't feel special.

Mediterranean choice
You can't go wrong with simple chicken, fish, vegetable and pasta dishes. They are healthy, varied, delicious and everyone loves them. Moreover, the majority of students are familiar with the food from this region.

Conclusion

_____

_____

C Read and complete the writing task below.

You are a member of the student council at an international college that hasn't got a canteen. The principal has asked you to write a proposal recommending whether the college should open a café, a bar or provide more vending machines.

Read the extract from the principal's email below. Then, write your proposal.

◀ ▶ email

From: principal@college.com
Sent: 19th April
Subject: College café, bar or vending machines

We need to decide whether the college should open a café, a bar or simply provide more vending machines in the common room.

café → hot beverages and food, soft drinks, somewhere to meet

bar → a fun place for students to meet in the evenings, music venue, no food, not appropriate for students under 18

more vending machines → food available at all times, not a healthy option, no hot food or beverages

Write your **proposal** in 180–220 words in an appropriate style.

Remember!
The main aim of a proposal is to put forward different options and persuade the reader to choose the option you think is best. Start by telling the reader why you are writing the proposal in your introduction. Describe the different options in your main paragraphs and then give your recommendation in your concluding paragraph. Make sure you use formal or semi-formal language, headings and discourse markers to add clarity and fluency to your writing. See the Writing Reference for proposals on page 179 of the Student's Book for further help.

Watch the clock!

 Spend 5 minutes reading the task and planning your proposal.

 Spend 30 minutes writing your proposal.

 Spend 5 minutes checking and editing your proposal.

Reading

Five paragraphs have been removed from the text. Choose from the paragraphs A–F the one which fits each gap (1–5). There is one extra paragraph which you do not need to use.

Building for Earthquakes

In earthquake-prone countries all over the world, billions of people live in houses that can't with stand shaking. Yet safer ones can be built cheaply – using straw, adobe and old tires – by applying a few general principles. **1**

But in less developed countries like Haiti, where a powerful quake in 2010 killed some 222,500 people and left more than a million homeless, conventional earthquake engineering is often unaffordable. 'The devastation in Haiti wouldn't happen in a developed country,' says engineer Marcial Blondet of the Catholic University of Peru, in Lima. Yet it needn't happen anywhere. Cheap solutions exist. **2**

Blondet's research team has found that existing adobe walls can be reinforced with a strong plastic mesh installed under plaster; in a quake, those walls crack but don't collapse, allowing occupants to escape. 'You rebuild your house, but you don't bury anyone,' Blondet says. Plastic mesh could also work as a reinforcement for concrete walls in Haiti and elsewhere. **3**

Such a house might be only a third as strong as one built on more sophisticated shock absorbers, but it would also cost much less – and so be more likely to get built in Indonesia. 'As an engineer you ask, What level of safety do I need? van de Lindt says. 'Then you look at what's actually available and find the solution somewhere in between.' **4**

The same stark contrast prevails in other fault zones. While the ideas may be encouraging, the progress is often discouraging. Even cheap ideas aren't always cheap enough. Since 2007 some 2,500 houses in Peru have been strengthened with plastic mesh or other reinforcements, with another 700 scheduled for this year. **5**

A This means that in Peru alone millions of houses still need to be built at a cost of billions of dollars. Many other countries are in a similar position. 'There are many millions of houses around the world,' Blondet says, 'that will collapse in the next earthquake.'

B In Los Angeles, Tokyo, and other rich cities in fault zones, the added expense of making buildings earthquake resistant has become a fact of life. Concrete walls are reinforced with steel, for instance, and a few buildings even rest on elaborate shock absorbers. Strict building codes were credited with saving thousands of lives when a magnitude 8.8 quake hit Chile.

C Some 80% of all the planet's earthquakes occur along the rim of the Pacific Ocean, called the 'Ring of Fire' because of the preponderance of volcanic activity there as well. Most earthquakes occur at fault zones, where tectonic plates – giant rock slabs that make up the Earth's upper layer – collide or slide against each other.

D Other engineers are working on methods that use local materials. Researchers in India have successfully tested a concrete house reinforced with bamboo. A model house for Indonesia rests on ground-motion dampers designed by John van de Lindt of Colorado State University: old tires filled with bags of sand.

E In northern Pakistan, straw is available. Traditional houses are built of stone and mud, but straw is far more resilient, says California engineer Darcey Donovan, and warmer in winter to boot. Donovan and her colleagues started building straw-bale houses in Pakistan after the 2005 earthquake; so far they have completed 17.

F Blondet has been working on ideas since 1970, when an earthquake in Peru killed 70,000 or more, many of whom died when their houses crumbled around them. Heavy, brittle walls of traditional adobe – cheap, sun-dried brick – cracked instantly when the ground started bucking. Subsequent shakes brought roofs thundering down.

Vocabulary

A Match the verbs 1–6 with the nouns and expressions a–f.

1 absorb ☐
2 emit ☐
3 endure ☐
4 harness ☐
5 spew ☐
6 trigger ☐

a energy
b oxygen
c ash and magma
d extreme weather conditions
e a landslide
f carbon-dioxide

B Complete the sentences with an expression from exercise A.

1 Because of global warming, we will have to _____ more frequently in future.
2 Heavy rainfall, cutting down trees, earthquakes and volcanic eruptions can all _____.
3 Unlike human beings who _____ through their lungs, fish use their gills.
4 Human beings _____ when they breathe out; plants then absorb it.
5 The Chilean volcano continues to _____, causing millions of dollars of damage.
6 We hope that in future we will _____ from the wind, the sun and ocean waves.

C Complete the text with these words.

barren breezy harsh hostile narrow searing steep sweltering

Desert wasteland

It was the most exhausting and difficult journey of their lives. Margot and Luke had set off at a vigorous pace, but it wasn't long before they were struggling as they climbed the **(1)** _____ slopes in the **(2)** _____ heat of the day. On and on they went along **(3)** _____, stony paths that made them trip and lose their balance. Then the landscape changed and they entered a **(4)** _____ region with no water or vegetation. It was **(5)** _____ for them in their long trousers and heavy walking boots, and they longed for a **(6)** _____ wind to cool them down. But as night fell, worse was to come. The temperature dropped and they had never felt so cold in their lives. Spending the night in such a **(7)** _____ place, listening to the howling of desert dogs and the scuttling of scorpions on the rocky ground, was a terrifying experience. For Margot, who had always thought of the desert as a **(8)** _____ but beautiful environment, it now felt like a bleak wasteland. She couldn't wait to get home!

D Complete the sentences with the correct form of the words in bold.

1 The weather is notoriously _____ in Scotland. You never know what to expect. **RELY**
2 Thankfully, there was _____ food to go around, so everyone survived the ordeal. **SUFFICE**
3 Birds undertake _____ in search of warmer weather and food. **MIGRATE**
4 They had a wonderful view of the _____ countryside from their hotel window. **SURROUND**
5 You need to make sure you wear adequate clothes to protect you from the _____. **ELEMENT**
6 Peter found his father's _____ on getting up before dawn quite exhausting. **INSIST**
7 I want to find an _____ to camping, but hotels are so expensive. **ALTER**
8 She walked on determinedly, _____ to the nasty, wet weather **DIFFER**

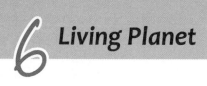

E Complete the sentences with *down*, *over* or *up*. Then underline the phrasal verbs.

1 It's bucketing _____! I'm not going out in this awful weather.

2 There was a terrible drought and rivers, lakes and wells dried _____.

3 It had been a wonderful day's sailing, then suddenly, a storm blew _____.

4 Do you think it will clear _____ soon? It's been raining since dawn.

5 The sun beat _____ on my head and I was so glad I had worn my hat after all.

6 What a relief! The storm has blown _____ and the damage has been minimal.

Grammar

A Complete the sentences with a positive or negative modal verb.

1 Seriously, you _____ go out and buy a new one. I've got two. You can have one of mine.

2 Twenty years ago, many girls in this region _____ read or write.

3 Before computers and video games, kids _____ spend hours reading or playing outside.

4 Does it rain much there at this time of the year? Do you think I _____ pack my waterproof?

5 This is a disaster. Something _____ be done to protect these animals or they will become extinct.

6 I've done everything you asked me to do. _____ I go and meet my friends now?

7 You _____ use your mobile phone in this carriage. It's not allowed.

8 You never know, it _____ snow, but it is quite unlikely at this time of the year.

B Complete the second sentences so that they have a similar meaning to the first sentences. Use the words in bold.

1 I'd like permission to leave now please. **may**
_____, please?

2 It isn't necessary to lock your doors here. It's very safe. **needn't**
You _____. It's very safe.

3 It isn't possible for Lucinda to be at home. I saw her a moment ago in that café. **can't**
Lucinda _____. I saw her a moment ago in that café.

4 It would be a good idea if you took the train, Jeremy. **could**
You _____, Jeremy.

5 I'm certain that Oscar will be late. He always is. **bound**
Oscar _____. He always is.

6 It isn't necessary to buy tickets in advance. There will be plenty on the day. **have to**
You _____. There will be plenty on the day.

7 If you want to be informed, I suggest you read this publication every week. **should**
You _____ every week if you want to be informed.

8 I am sure that your keys are somewhere in the house. **must**
Your keys _____ the house.

C Complete the sentences with the correct modal perfect form of the verbs in brackets.

1 There isn't any milk! The children _____ (finish) it this morning at breakfast.

2 I'm not sure, but I think I _____ (leave) my gloves on the bus yesterday.

3 Anna was concerned about the kids, but she _____ (worry) as they were fine.

4 We _____ (give) you a lift if we'd known you were coming.

5 Seriously, she _____ (tidy) her room. It's still a terrible mess.

6 I'm exhausted! It's my own fault, though. I _____ (go) to bed so late last night.

D Circle the correct words.

The extinction of the dinosaurs

There are many theories as to why dinosaurs became extinct. One of the most popular today is the Asteroid theory. This states that the dinosaurs **(1)** must become / **must have become** extinct when a huge asteroid hit Earth. The asteroid **(2)** would throw / **would have thrown** enormous amounts of dust into the air and plunged the world into darkness. Because plants can't grow without light, the dinosaurs **(3)** **must have starved** / can't have starved to death. Another theory suggests that it was a dramatic increase in volcanic activity 65 million years ago that caused the mass extinction. Each volcano **(4)** should have spewed / **would have spewed** so much magma and ash in the atmosphere that few animals and plants **(5)** **could have survived** / needn't have survived. Others believe a prolonged ice age **(6)** **might have been** / ought to have been the cause. The dinosaurs **(7)** **wouldn't have been able** / must have been able to survive in such low temperatures. Yet another possibility is that a deadly disease **(8)** can't have spread / **may have spread** amongst the dinosaurs and ended up causing their demise. We will never know for sure.

E Match the sentences 1–5 with an appropriate response a–e.

1 It's cold outside and they're freezing! ☐
2 Their passports are still here. ☐
3 She had prepared a fantastic meal for them. ☐
4 Oh, dear! The children aren't on this train. ☐
5 Mark and Henry are completely lost. ☐

a They must have missed it.
b They should have brought their coats.
c They needn't have brought their own lunch.
d They ought to have taken a map.
e They can't have gone abroad.

Listening

You will hear two different extracts. For questions 1–4, choose the best answer, a, b or c. There are two questions for each extract.

Extract One

You will hear two people talking about bush fires.

1 What did the man know that the woman hadn't known about?
   a There aren't many bush fires in Australia.
   b Forest fires are actually quite common.
   c Firefighters often use fire to put out forest fires.

2 What do both speakers agree about?
   a Forest fires are sometimes necessary.
   b Carelessness causes fires in four out of five cases.
   c These days, fires are managed better than they were before.

Extract Two

You will hear two people discussing the habits of the parasitic emerald cockroach wasp.

3 Why is the cockroach wasp extraordinary?
   a The female lays her eggs on the body of another insect.
   b The larva buries itself inside the cockroach as it is safe there.
   c The wasp larva uses its own secretions to clean the cockroach.

4 What do the wasp larva secretions consist of?
   a antibiotic liquids that kill the cockroach
   b chemicals needed to kill harmful substances in the cockroach
   c an antiseptic and antifungal liquid that cleans up its food

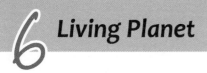

writing

A Read the writing task below and write T (true) or F (false).

> *You have been asked to write a contribution to a volunteering website, which lists different volunteering projects worldwide and encourages young people to give up some of their time to help out on a particular project.*
>
> *Your contribution should:*
>
> - *describe a particular project run by volunteers in your country*
> - *list the tasks you expect volunteers to take on*
> - *describe the kind of person project leaders are looking for*
> - *show how volunteers will benefit from volunteering.*

1 You should write in a formal, official style. ☐

2 You should be honest about how much hard work you'll expect. ☐

3 You needn't be specific about who should apply to volunteer. ☐

4 You should mention how volunteers can enjoy their spare time. ☐

B Read the model contribution and complete it with these verbs in the correct form.

aim   dispose   improve   include   save   thrive

Project: Save our Native Birds

We are a volunteer-run conservation project which **(1)** _____ to stop the decline in the population of some of our best-loved native birds. We are involved in improving their natural habitat so that these birds can **(2)** _____ once more.

The contribution of our volunteers is essential in making the project work. Tasks could **(3)** _____ two or more of the following:

- collecting seeds
- **(4)** _____ of litter
- emptying bins
- filling up bird feeders
- checking nests

We are looking for young people between the ages of 18 and 25 who are hard-working and committed **(5)** _____ our native birds. No experience is needed, only enthusiasm, a wish to learn and a wish to make a difference.

It won't all be hard work on *Project: Save our Native Birds*! There will be plenty of time to go swimming in the crystal clear river and to trek in the forest. And of course, you will be doing lots of bird watching. Best of all, you will meet and spend time with other like-minded young people and make friendships that will last a lifetime.

Do join us for an unforgettable two weeks! You will help **(6)** _____ our world and have a wonderful time doing it.

C **Read and complete the writing task below.**

You have been asked to write a contribution to an international magazine about a volunteering project in your country. Your contribution should:

- *describe the aims of the volunteering project*
- *explain what sort of work the project needs volunteers to do*
- *describe the ideal volunteer*
- *conclude by describing the benefits to both volunteers and the project.*

*Write your **contribution** in 220–260 words in an appropriate style.*

Watch the clock!

 Spend 5 minutes reading the task and planning your contribution.

 Spend 30 minutes writing your contribution.

 Spend 5 minutes checking and editing your contribution.

Vocabulary

A Choose the correct answers.

1 You won't ___ your thirst by drinking more coffee.
   a rid
   b shed
   c quench
   d fulfill

2 Don't give him crisps. They're too ___ for children.
   a salty
   b sour
   c sweet
   d bitter

3 Can I use the ___ from lunch to make myself a snack?
   a scraps
   b coverings
   c extracts
   d leftovers

4 Would you like a second ___ of lasagna?
   a help
   b helping
   c cover
   d service

5 Stir the coffee well until the sugar is ___.
   a softened
   b dissolved
   c melted
   d blanched

6 Dinner is on the table. Come and tuck ___.
   a out
   b up
   c in
   d off

7 There are no chocolates. Who polished them ___?
   a up
   b away
   c out
   d off

8 These genetically ___ tomatoes don't have seeds.
   a modified
   b varied
   c changed
   d revised

9 Eating nothing but junk food can lead to ___.
   a famine
   b underfeeding
   c malnutrition
   d starvation

10 You can't have your cake and ___ it, too.
   a consume
   b gobble
   c eat
   d scoff

11 Plants ___ carbon dioxide and emit oxygen.
   a attract
   b receive
   c consume
   d absorb

12 It rarely pours, but it's often very ___ in this area.
   a sprinkly
   b drizzly
   c torrential
   d dusty

13 This heat is very ___ here in summer.
   a oppressed
   b oppressive
   c depressed
   d depressive

14 The harsh midday sun has ___ the emerging seedlings.
   a parched
   b saturated
   c scorched
   d shrunken

15 Heavy rain caused the deadly ___.
   a landslide
   b landfall
   c landfill
   d landscape

16 We are ___ on you to bring the food for the picnic.
   a trusting
   b confiding
   c hoping
   d relying

17 I hope it clears ___ in time for our barbecue tonight.
   a on
   b over
   c up
   d away

18 The authorities are ___ to the refugees' plight.
   a indifferent
   b ignorant
   c uncaring
   d merciless

19 Don't let gaming interfere ___ your homework.
   a in
   b on
   c from
   d with

20 Why do you insist ___ leaving now. It's still early.
   a in
   b on
   c by
   d against

Grammar

B **Choose the correct answers.**

1 We've decided ___ of red meat we eat every week.
   a to cut on the quantity down
   b to cut the quantity down on
   c to cut down on the quantity
   d the quantity to cut down on

2 I spilt my drink and had to ___.
   a it clean up
   b clean up it
   c up clean it
   d clean it up

3 We'll ___ until tomorrow.
   a put it off
   b put off it
   c off put it
   d off it put

4 They ___ during their journey.
   a came many obstacles up against
   b came up many obstacles against
   c many obstacles came up against
   d came up against many obstacles

5 So you think it's all over, ___?
   a are you?
   b isn't it?
   c do you?
   d you don't?

6 I don't suppose I could hand it in tomorrow, ___?
   a could I
   b couldn't I
   c do I
   d suppose I

7 That's a fantastic book, ___.
   a is that
   b that is
   c isn't that
   d that isn't

8 You wouldn't be able to give me lift, ___?
   a you would
   b you wouldn't
   c would you
   d wouldn't you

9 She'll never finish it, ___?
   a will she
   b won't she
   c isn't she
   d hasn't she

10 He ___ the message. He'd be here if he had.
   a can't get
   b couldn't get
   c can't have got
   d can't be getting

11 The car isn't in the drive. Dave ___.
   a must take it
   b must have taken it
   c needn't take it
   d has to take it

12 You really ___ late or they'll go without you.
   a won't be
   b wouldn't be
   c could have been
   d mustn't be

13 ___ some more onions, or have we got enough?
   a Should I get
   b Would I get
   c Would I have got
   d Needn't I get

14 It's a very good make. It ___ to last a lifetime.
   a should
   b ought
   c must
   d bound

15 It ___ work, but let's hope it does.
   a couldn't
   b mustn't
   c might not
   d wouldn't

16 The appointment isn't today. It ___ yesterday.
   a must be
   b must have been
   c would have been
   d should be

17 I can't find my glasses. I ___ them on the train.
   a can't leave
   b can't have left
   c might leave
   d might have left

18 They ___ to get in. It's free.
   a don't have to pay
   b mustn't pay
   c would have paid
   d could have paid

19 You ___ into your uniform. Nobody else has.
   a needed to change
   b can't have changed
   c needn't have changed
   d couldn't have changed

20 He ___ there. It was so much fun!
   a should be
   b should have been
   c must be
   d mustn't be

Use of English

C Choose the correct answer.

The Mediterranean way

There is more evidence proving the Mediterranean diet to be heart healthy and most likely helpful in **(1)** ___ pounds and keeping them off. Although Mediterranean **(2)** ___ is not technically low in fat, the type of **(3)** ___ acids it does contain, such as those that come from nuts and olive oil, is a much healthier form of **(4)** ___ fat than what exists in other foods. In a recent study, participants who were overweight and suffering from **(5)** ___ were placed on either a regular low-fat diet or a Mediterranean diet. The ones on the latter diet fared better than their counterparts in terms of health risks. The results showed that it is not just a matter of eating low-fat **(6)** ___ of food, but it is the addition of nuts and olive oil that improves the indicators of good health. The ones who followed the regular low-fat diet also **(7)** ___ the risk of returning to old habits that caused them to **(8)** ___ on the pounds in the first place. A Mediterranean diet is easier to follow because it is filled with healthy yet **(9)** ___ foods such as fish, walnuts and fresh fruit and vegetables. Those who follow the diet are less likely to suffer from **(10)** ___ for less healthier foods, thus making it easier to **(11)** ___ the urge to eat meat and high-fat dairy products. Ultimately, the Mediterranean diet contains all the nutrients needed for lifelong health, making it a diet people can **(12)** ___ on for their entire lives.

		a	**b**	**c**	**d**
1		scraping	shredding	shedding	cracking
2		feast	cuisine	platter	spread
3		fattening	fat	fatty	fattened
4		diet	dieting	dietician	dietary
5		obesity	disorder	malnutrition	indigestion
6		toppings	servings	coverings	flavourings
7		packed	ran	played	quenched
8		stuff	stack	place	pile
9		sharp	bitter	bland	appetising
10		cravings	passions	urges	appetites
11		whip	resist	polish	feed
12		live	dine	pick	tuck

D Complete the text by writing one word in each gap.

Wild and windy

Could you imagine living where winds exceed 240 kilometres per hour? It wouldn't be easy, **(1)** _____ it? To do so, you would **(2)** _____ to travel to Commonwealth Bay, Antarctica, Earth's windiest place. The bay's winds are created by storms that blow **(3)** _____ suddenly and push air down the bay's slopes. Even more unusual is the storm clouds often **(4)** _____ up just as quickly as they form, allowing the sun to beat **(5)** _____ on the region again just minutes after being hidden. Ships are advised **(6)** _____ travelling through the bay, and surely any captain that insisted **(7)** _____ travelling through it **(8)** _____ risk crashing, or even vanishing **(9)** _____ thin air! In this hostile **(10)** _____ breathtaking area, there are more than a few signs of **(11)** _____. Travellers to the region are **(12)** _____ to see penguins in the snow. These birds **(13)** _____ nature thrive in cold weather and remain seemingly unaware **(14)** _____ Earth's calmer climates. With winds like those at Commonwealth Bay, however, it's hard to see how they don't blow away, isn't **(15)** _____?

E **Think of one word only that can be used appropriately in all three sentences.**

1 Marie lightly used her _____ to get her horse moving along.

If you're completely starving, I can _____ something up in a few minutes.

You will need to _____ the cream for a while to get it thick.

2 Mark had to get up at 6am to give the cattle their _____.

Michelle enrolled in cooking school to _____ her passion for cooking.

Bacteria _____ off the sun's energy in order to grow and multiply.

3 See if you can _____ the text quickly and find the main idea.

There's a bit of dirt floating in the water, but you should be able to _____ it off the top.

There was a _____ of ice on the dish when I took it out of the fridge.

4 I told you to keep this a secret – why did you _____ the beans?

There was a tragic oil _____ in the ocean near the coast of Spain.

Sheila was riding her bike dangerously and took a nasty _____.

5 This new restaurant isn't the only one of its kind – it's part of a larger _____.

Scientists were able to put together the _____ of events that caused the disaster.

Lisa used a lock and _____ to secure her bike to the lamp post.

F **Complete the second sentences so that they have a similar meaning to the first sentences using the words in bold. Use between three and six words.**

1 It must have been raining heavily last night.

BUCKETING

The rain _____ hours last night.

2 It could be possible that scientists didn't know oxygen existed back then.

MIGHT

Scientists _____ that oxygen existed back then.

3 We must stay away from the animals while they're sleeping.

INTERFERE

We _____ the animals while they're sleeping.

4 It was completely unnecessary to attend the meeting.

WASTE

It was _____ to attend the meeting.

5 Mike couldn't have eaten everything on his plate.

POLISHED

There's no way Mike _____ the food on his plate.

6 Mary told her not to bother getting upset about the situation.

MILK

Regarding the situation, Mary told her there was _____.

7 I can't figure out how they stand to be around him.

PUT

I can't understand how they _____.

8 You have to realise there's a problem that needs to be dealt with.

WAKE

In regards to the problem at hand, you _____ coffee.

Eureka!

Reading

Read the article and answer the questions.

IF WE HAD WINGS...

A Perched on the edge of a cold, windswept dune in North Carolina, I was about to fulfill a dream I shared with Leonardo da Vinci: to fly. The Renaissance genius spent years deciphering the flight of birds and devising flying machines. On his deathbed in 1519, Leonardo said one of his regrets was that he had never flown. Five hundred years of innovation since then had produced the hang glider I held above my head, simple and safe enough to be offered as a tourist entertainment. But despite centuries of adventure and experimentation, personal flight remains elusive.

B Leonardo drew hundreds of images of birds on the wing, trying to decode their secrets, and drew meticulous plans for flying machines not unlike today's gliders and helicopters. But he never figured out the physics of flight. It took more than 300 years and many more failed experiments until Sir George Cayley, a British engineer, determined that flight required lift, propulsion, and control. He built a glider with a curved wing to create lift. It gained enough speed to fly but crashed after only a few hundred yards.

C The best success in purely human-powered flight came in 1988, when the *Daedalus*, a lightweight aircraft built by a team at the Massachusetts Institute of Technology, flew 71.5 miles from the Greek island of Crete to Santorini. The 69-pound craft, pedalled by a Greek Olympic cyclist, got caught in turbulence as it approached the beach at Santorini. It crashed in the sea, a few yards from the shore.

D Inventors continue to try to bring the fantasy of personal flight to life, and Yves Rossy has come closest. This Swiss pilot flings himself out of an aircraft wearing a six-foot-wide carbon-fiber wing of his own invention, powered by four tiny jet engines. Recently, Rossy jumped from a helicopter above the Grand Canyon in the USA and flew for eight minutes before parachuting to Earth. The jets give him the power to ascend and to do loops. That freedom doesn't come easy; it took Rossy years to master his tiny craft. 'I steer myself in space with only my body,' he explains. 'To go left, I turn my shoulders left, and that's it!' He says it's like parachuting with a wing suit.

E You won't catch me jumping out of a plane with a wing strapped to my back. But I yearn for even a small measure of Rossy's joy in flight. After five attempts from one of the highest sand dunes in the eastern USA last April, I was getting closer – able to fly into the wind, then float gently down onto my feet. It was as if the glider wasn't there.

F But I wanted more. Sandra Vernon, a 47-year-old mother of three in my class on the dune, egged me on. She'd been flying towed tandem flights, pulled 2,000 feet behind an ultralight aircraft. This usually gives a hang glider a good ten-minute flight back down to Earth, even if there is no rising warm air to help keep the craft up. 'I'm short, I'm chubby, I'm not spry,' Vernon says. 'I wish I had been doing this in my 20s. You can't help but love it.'

G Challenge accepted, I strapped myself into the harness of a tandem glider with my instructor. He warned me that the moment when the plane released us would remind me of going over the top of a roller coaster. I'm a coaster fan. This was nothing like that. It felt like falling headfirst off the top of a 2,000-foot-tall building. 'You can fly now,' he said, offering me the controls. 'No!' I shouted over the wind. In a few moments the glider began to rise and then fly horizontally. My terror lessened, and I took control. I moved to the left, then to the right – more of a pigeon than an eagle but flying all the same.

In which section are the following mentioned?

improving one's performance with practice	1	☐
flying with an experienced professional	2	☐
the first glider ever to fly a short distance	3	☐
disappointment over an unfulfilled dream	4	☐
a great deal of time to learn how to do something	5	☐
longing for the same experience as another person	6	☐
a flying machine powered by human legs	7	☐
encouraging someone to try something new	8	☐
someone experiencing great fear	9	☐
flying apparatus powered by fuel	10	☐

Vocabulary

A Choose the correct answers.

1 Unfortunately, solar power isn't cost- ___ unless you live in a sunny part of the world.
   a capable   b effective   c valuable

2 I'm afraid my diet was rather ___. I was too hungry to keep it up for more than a couple of days.
   a short-term   b long-lasting   c short-lived

3 Andrea's report was ___. I couldn't have explained the situation any better.
   a spotless   b spot on   c spotty

4 Because polystyrene is such a poor ___ of heat, it is the ideal material for disposable coffee cups.
   a conductor   b conduit   c mediator

5 The statistical ___ made it difficult to compare the data from one year to the next.
   a variety   b anomaly   c inconsistency

6 They didn't want to ___ his scientific theory even though it was contradictory.
   a dispose   b refuse   c discard

7 Did you bring any eating ___ or are we going to have to use our fingers?
   a forks   b utensils   c tools

8 Newborn babies shouldn't feed from bottles that haven't been ___.
   a sterilised   b contaminated   c refreshed

B Complete the sentences with the correct form of the words.

1 _____ is responsible for many of the changes we've seen in the last 100 years.
2 In order to determine the _____ of a substance, you'll need to carry out tests.
3 The invention of the _____ line revolutionised the manufacturing industry.
4 The formation of rust on iron is one of the most familiar examples of _____.
5 Archimedes discovered the principle of liquid _____ when he was having a bath.
6 These days, _____ sewing machines can embroider clothes in minutes.
7 My grandmother recovered from her hip _____ surgery very quickly.
8 Making quick _____ about people can lead to injustice and should be avoided.

AUTOMATE
PURE
ASSEMBLE
CORRODE
DISPLACE
COMPUTER
REPLACE
ASSUME

C Circle the correct words in the text.

Synthetic diamonds

Few people have heard of scientist Dr Tracy Hall, who died in 2008. In 1954, he and three colleagues at the General Electric Research Laboratory in New York did something extraordinary. They managed to create a diamond using a **(1)** material / matter called graphite, a form of carbon that is used in pencils. The procedure they followed was similar to the natural **(2)** practice / process, which would have taken place deep in the earth, millions of years ago. By using very high temperatures and man-made pressure on graphite, they managed to produce a **(3)** solution / substance that had all the **(4)** phenomena / properties of diamonds. These synthetic or man-made diamonds are in fact identical to real diamonds, possessing the same **(5)** hardness / harshness and transparency as the real thing. Today, synthetic diamonds are used to coat equipment used for cutting, like saws, grinding wheels and mining drills. These **(6)** artificial / pretend diamonds are cheaper than real diamonds, though it is still very expensive to produce a large synthetic diamond which can be used as a **(7)** gemstone / jewellery. Although Dr Hall never received the Nobel Prize for his invention, within the huge and thriving artificial diamond **(8)** factory / industry, he is rightly considered as the father of the synthetic diamond.

D **Complete the words in the sentences.**

1 On a newspaper's website you can read all of the headlines on the h_ _ _ p_ _ _ .
2 I accidentally deleted the file, but luckily it was still in the r_ _ _ _ _ _ b _ _.
3 I don't know what we'd do without s_ _ _ _ _ e_ _ _ _ _ _ like Google and Yahoo for looking things up on the web.
4 If you d_ _ _ _ _ c_ _ _ _ on this icon at the top, it will send you to the right web page.
5 I've just bought a new external h_ _ _ d_ _ _ _, which has a very big storage capacity.
6 This l_ _ _ _ p_ _ _ _ _ _ is much quicker and the quality is better than my old ink-jet printer.
7 Copy your photos onto your m_ _ _ _ _ s_ _ _ _ and you can take them to be developed in town.
8 To add or remove a program from your computer, just go to the c_ _ _ _ _ _ p_ _ _ _ and click on 'Programs'.

E **Match the first parts of the sentences 1–6 to the second parts a–f.**

1 They should have kept calm, but they ☐
2 Their company is light years ahead ☐
3 Look, it's not rocket science. ☐
4 We got our wires crossed and I ☐
5 Why reinvent the wheel when ☐
6 This really is cutting edge technology! ☐

a ended up waiting in the wrong restaurant.
b I've never seen anything like it.
c in terms of technological innovation.
d this system works perfectly?
e All you have to do is change the batteries.
f pushed the panic button instead.

Grammar

A **Complete the conditional sentences with the verbs in brackets in the correct form.**

1 Sophie wouldn't have got a place at university if she _____ such good grades in her exams. (get)
2 You _____ your exam unless you are prepared to do lots of revision. (pass)
3 Honestly, if I _____ you, I would, but I'm broke at the moment. (help)
4 Even if Benjamin Franklin hadn't been one of the Founding Fathers of the United States, he _____ famous today for his many inventions. (still be)
5 If Joseph hadn't studied chemistry at university, it's unlikely that he _____ the well-paid job he's now had for ten years. (get)
6 Do you think the world would be a better place if Leo Baekeland _____ plastic? (never invent)
7 I can't imagine what my life _____ like if labour-saving devices like the vacuum cleaner and the microwave oven hadn't been invented. (be)
8 If you _____ vinegar and bicarbonate of soda, it fizzes. (mix)

B Circle the correct words in the text.

A cure for malaria

Over one million people die of malaria every year and more than half a billion are infected with the disease. But what can be done to prevent it? And what are your chances **(1)** if / unless you do contract the disease?

Prevention is better than cure and **(2)** if / unless you are bitten by a malaria-carrying mosquito, you won't get malaria. So, **(3)** as long as / supposing you take anti-malaria tablets and use a good insect repellent, and **(4)** provided / but for you always sleep under a mosquito net in high-risk malaria regions, you should be able to prevent getting the disease, although you **(5)** will / won't be able to do away with the risk altogether.

(6) Otherwise / Supposing you did contract malaria, despite taking every precaution, what would happen then? You would have to take very strong drugs or **(7)** otherwise / provided you might not survive. Unfortunately, these drugs **(8)** would / wouldn't almost certainly make you feel a lot worse before you felt any better. There is hope, however, that a single-dose cure with almost no side effects will soon be available. Researchers in South Africa believe they have discovered a drug that is able to kill the parasite instantly. **(9)** If / Unless this proves to be the case, it **(10)** can / could transform the lives of people living in high-risk regions.

C Match the first parts of the sentences 1–8 to the second parts a–h.

1 If you put a cold egg in boiling water, ☐
2 Epidemics of diphtheria and whooping cough would be common today ☐
3 Michael might not have survived such an infection ☐
4 You must add yeast to the flour mixture, ☐
5 Had I known the professor was going to be giving the lecture, ☐
6 You must realise the experiment will fail ☐
7 Provided you don't overwater them, ☐
8 Hold the jar for me ☐

a if children weren't immunised as babies.
b unless all the conditions are perfect.
c otherwise your bread won't rise.
d and I'll pour the liquid into it.
e it often cracks.
f your houseplants will thrive.
g I would certainly have gone to it.
h but for the large doses of antibiotics he was given in hospital.

D Complete the second sentences so that they have a similar meaning to the first sentences.

1 Hannah is always late. It's very annoying.
   I wish _____.
2 Daniel didn't revise for the test. He regrets this now.
   Daniel wishes _____.
3 The fact that I'll never be a musician makes me quite sad.
   If only _____.
4 Henry is upset because he isn't going on holiday with his friends.
   Henry wishes _____.
5 You never do the washing-up! It's so irritating.
   I wish _____ once in a while.

E Rewrite the sentences using inversion.

1 This book is extremely long and it's very boring.

Not only _____, but _____.

2 You won't find a more patient teacher anywhere.

Nowhere _____.

3 We were hardly ever allowed to do experiments when we were children.

Rarely _____ when we were children.

4 I had to wait until I was thirty before being able to afford a car.

Not until _____ to afford to buy a car.

5 The minute they got to the beach they ran into the sea.

No sooner _____ than _____.

6 You're not to lift this by yourself as it's much too heavy.

Under no circumstances _____ as it's much too heavy.

Listening

You will hear a presentation about how technology is changing the lives of people in Africa. Listen and complete sentences 1–8.

1 The report is about how _____ have transformed life for ordinary people in Africa.

2 In some African countries more than half of all adults use mobiles when making _____ transactions.

3 Mobile phones are helping to create openness and _____ in elections.

4 Compared to personal computers, mobile phones are _____ and easier to use for students.

5 Nigerians use their phones to send in their votes for _____ shows on television.

6 Refugee databases provide information that can _____ family members.

7 Farmers are able to share information about the _____.

8 Unique codes on packaging will enable people to check whether a medicine is _____.

Writing

A Read the writing task below and answer the questions.

You see the following announcement in a college science magazine.

> ### Most influential medical researcher
>
> *We are planning an issue about the most influential medical researchers of all time. Which person would you nominate to be included in the issue? Write to us describing this person's achievements and explaining why you feel he or she should be included.*

1 Who will be judging your nomination?
2 What will you be writing about?
3 Do you have to write about researchers in the 21st century?
4 What sort of language should you use?

B The paragraphs in the model competition entry are in the wrong order. Put the paragraphs in the correct order, 1–4.

Edward Jenner – inventor of the vaccination

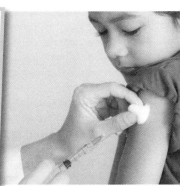

_____ Edward Jenner is regarded as the inventor of the smallpox vaccine and the father of immunology. He created the first vaccine in 1776. Today, smallpox has been eradicated from our planet and we have vaccinations for almost all dangerous diseases.

_____ It is easy to forget that before immunisation, parents didn't expect all their children to survive into adulthood and were terrified of diseases we are unfamiliar with now. But today, thanks to improved living conditions and medical advances like immunisation and antibiotics, the vast majority of parents can expect their children to thrive. Scientists like Edward Jenner led the way.

_____ Two hundred years ago, if you contracted a disease like smallpox or cholera, you would be lucky to survive. Today, thanks to immunisation, you are unlikely to be exposed to them, and if you were, you'd be protected against them thanks to the vaccinations you got as an infant. We have Dr Edward Jenner to thank for this.

_____ Jenner used experiments to prove his theories about smallpox. He had observed that people who had had cowpox never got smallpox and so he concluded that this was what gave them immunity. He tested it on his own baby son and other children. He inserted cowpox into a small cut on their arms. They then got the milder cowpox disease, but became immune to the real killer, smallpox. Jenner published his results and called the procedure vaccination from the Latin word 'vacca', meaning cow. It was the beginning of immunisation.

C Read and complete the writing task below.

You see the following announcement in an international newspaper.

> *Who has made the greatest technological or scientific discoveries in the last 50 years? Write and tell us who you believe this person is, what they have achieved and why their contribution is so important. The best entries will be published in the next issue.*

*Write your **competition entry** in 220–260 words in an appropriate style.*

Remember!

In a competition entry, your aim is to persuade the reader that your nomination is the best one. Start by giving a general description and follow on by providing a more detailed portrayal and assessment of the person's achievements. Make sure you finish with a persuasive final paragraph. See the Writing Reference for competition entries on page 181 of the Student's Book for further help.

Watch the clock!

 Spend 5 minutes reading the task and planning your competition entry.

 Spend 30 minutes writing your competition entry.

 Spend 5 minutes checking and editing your competition entry.

Reading

Read the article and choose the answer (a, b, c or d) which fits best according to the text.

The invisible bank

In the developed world, we are used to the idea that we created the model of industrial and economic progress which other countries must follow. Many of our big ideas about development rest on the assumption that the West cracked the formula for economic progress sometime in the 19th century, and what we need now is for the developing world to 'catch up'. Even the language we use encapsulates this idea, in the division between 'developed' and 'developing'. But new innovations are challenging the idea that development requires handing ideas down from developed to developing. In banking and finance, the big ideas in cashless transfers and mobile, flexible exchanges are not to be found in Geneva or London or New York. A revolution in mobile money transfer has occurred, but not in these financial centres. Instead, it's happened in Kenya, with m-Pesa.

The service was developed between Safaricom and Vodafone, and launched in 2007. And it's not just something used in cities or by big commercial interests. By 2010, over 50% of Kenya's population had used it – this means rural villagers haggling over produce, then using their Nokias to make the final deal. It means Masai herdsmen bringing their phones to market along with their cattle, ready to stock up on essentials to bring back to their homes.

For people who live in isolated areas, the service means no longer having to carry lots of cash to markets or towns, risking losing huge amounts to banditry and theft. For people without permanent addresses or bank accounts, the service means they can pay what cash they have to m-Pesa in exchange for mobile credit, making payments and transfers and building up savings – becoming participants in an economy from which they had previously been locked out. For migrants, the service allows them to send money home to their families and villages safely and simply. Safaricom's international money transfer service uses a similar system for international immigrants, coordinating great webs of remittances and payments across the world. For Kenyan businesses, the service means payments for stock or repairs can happen almost instantaneously, wiping out the need to rely on bank clearances and flawed infrastructure which had clogged the economy with inefficiencies and delays.

So how does it work? m-Pesa relies on a network of small shop-front retailers, who register to be m-Pesa agents. Customers come to these retailers and pay them cash in exchange for loading virtual credit onto their phone, known as e-float. E-float can be swapped and transferred between mobile users with a simple text message and a system of codes. The recipient of e-float takes her mobile phone into her nearest retailer when she wants to cash in, and swaps her text message code back for physical money. There are already more m-Pesa agents in Kenya than there are bank branches.

Such a system also requires intermediaries, to get the cash to m-Pesa agents, and ensure cash movement keeps up with e-float exchanges. In this way, the system has created new jobs, with some intermediaries and retailers earning $1,000 a month in commission from m-Pesa transactions.

As of m-Pesa's fifth birthday – March 6 2012 – it had been used by a staggering 15 million people. The system was employed by the 'Kenyans for Kenya' campaign to raise money for Kenyans suffering from the Horn of Africa drought – just one way in which it has contributed to independence and innovation in Kenya's economy.

In response to m-Pesa's success, the model has been imitated in other countries. Africa's biggest mobile operator MTN has rolled out schemes elsewhere, the most ambitious in Kenya's neighbour Uganda. Central banks in some countries, such as Brazil, have now created financial inclusion teams, with a vision for using similar systems to bring financial access to the poor and isolated. The Indian government has also shown determination to achieve this aim, and analysts predict, with its strong IT infrastructure and dense population, India too could be on the road to becoming a cash-light, financially inclusive economy in the near future.

1 The writer believes that economic progress
   a is taking place in major financial centres.
   b has yet to occur in developing countries.
   c is happening in unexpected places.
   d is only possible with mobile transactions.

2 The majority of Kenyans
   a are involved in commerce.
   b have made business deals on their mobile phones.
   c exchange goods at markets.
   d have made a cashless transaction.

3 Transferring money via mobile phones is
   a more efficient than old-fashioned banking services.
   b risky due to an increase in crime.
   c impracticable for homeless people.
   d an inefficient method for sending money abroad.

4 The typical m-Pesa agent
   a works in a bank.
   b is a financial broker.
   c is a village, town or city shopkeeper.
   d does all his or her business online.

5 The mobile phone money transfer system
   a has replaced the banks in Kenya.
   b has cost as much as $1,000 a month.
   c ensures that less cash is distributed in the country.
   d has led to the generation of new jobs in Kenya.

6 The m-Pesa system has been used
   a to increase people's independence.
   b to help people affected by a natural disaster.
   c to modernise the economic and political system.
   d for five years.

Vocabulary

A Complete the text with these words.

> bank teller   cash   counterfeit   currency   dollars   forgeries   money   pounds

The forgery

I was on holiday in New York a few weeks ago and came home to London with about seventy **(1)** _____ in **(2)** _____ that I hadn't spent while I was there. Yesterday, I finally took the **(3)** _____ to a bank to change it into **(4)** _____ .

When I passed the notes to the **(5)** _____ , I noticed that he looked at each of them very carefully. Then he examined them all under a special light on his desk. I asked him if there was a problem.

'These two notes are **(6)** _____ ,' he said, holding them up. 'I'm sorry but I'm afraid I can't exchange them for you and the bank will have to hand them over to the police.'

I was naturally quite shocked and upset. He apologised again but went on to explain that there had been a recent surge in the number of **(7)** _____ notes detected, all in American **(8)** _____ .

B The words in bold are in the wrong form. Write the correct form next to each sentence.

1 Delia hadn't realised Bernie had been involved in **fraud** business practices. _____
2 If you don't stop spending at such a rate, you're going to end up **broken**. _____
3 Melissa decided to **withdrawal** all the money she had in the account and then closed it. _____
4 Money **laundry** involves hiding money which has been obtained illegally. _____
5 It is more **economic** to boil water in an electric kettle than in a pan on the stove. _____
6 Many people thought that **poor** would be a thing of the past by the 21st century. _____
7 Countries around the world have been affected by the **recess**, even the wealthiest ones. _____
8 The country's credit **rate** has been downgraded, and the government can't borrow money. _____

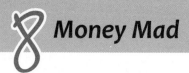

C Match the sentences 1–6 to the sentences a–f.

1 We have inherited a fortune! ☐
2 For my money, this is the best cafe in town. ☐
3 You won't get your money's worth if you buy it. ☐
4 Stop throwing money at this project. ☐
5 Why does he throw his money around? ☐
6 Babysitting is easy money when kids behave. ☐

a The food is great and it's reasonable.
b Doesn't he know people are struggling?
c But it's different when they're difficult!
d We're in the money, so let's celebrate.
e You should just cut your losses.
f It's badly made and overpriced.

D Circle the correct words.

1 There's no way you can live by / on $100 a week. It's impossible if you're paying rent.
2 Listen, if we all chip in / out we'll be able to take Dad out for his birthday. He'd love that, you know.
3 Oh, dear. This is going to set you back / forwards a few pennies. Do you really think you can afford it?
4 Come on, splash out / up for once in your life. You know you want to and you can certainly afford it!
5 I can't believe you expect me to fork in / out $50 for this t-shirt. I don't care how fashionable it is, I'm not buying it.
6 We're so excited! We've put back / down a deposit for the apartment and we'll be moving in next month.

Grammar

A Complete the text with the best phrase (a–j).

a whose lives have been turned _____
b where no borrowing, bartering or sales _____
c where you can find stuff for free _____
d which is the first step _____
e when we realise that getting used stuff _____

f which will cost no more than $25 _____
g who see no need to buy brand-new clothing _____
h which are going to cost you $200 _____
i who want to trade _____
j who live in your neighbourhood _____

How to cope in tough times

No one can argue that a recession is a good thing, but recessions do force us to re-evaluate where, and how, we spend our money, **(1)** _____ on the path to a more environmentally-friendly way of life. Do you really need a new pair of boots, **(2)** _____, or could you just fix the heels on your old ones, **(3)** _____? Sites **(4)** _____ are rapidly turning the Internet from a global yellow pages into the world's largest swap meet, making our consumer habits vastly greener and more budget-friendly. People **(5)** _____ upside down by the recession are finding new ways of getting by. Not only can you buy items more cheaply online, you can also exchange and borrow. Sites like Neighborrow.com let you post items you'd like to lend to, or borrow or buy from, people **(6)** _____. They've even organised borrowing sites for university students **(7)** _____ textbooks. Likewise, handmedowns.com is aimed at mums and mums-to-be **(8)** _____ and gear for kids that grow out of things fast. If borrowing in cyberspace doesn't work for you, contact the founders of really.reallyfree.org for tips on how to organise a neighbourhood giveaway, **(9)** _____ are allowed, just honest handouts of stuff you no longer find useful. The world and our landfills are full of top-quality, slightly used goods. A recession shouldn't be the only time **(10)** _____ for free isn't just economical, it's the greenest thing you can do.

B Choose the correct answers.

1 I bought this bike second-hand from Stephen, ___ you met last week at the garage sale.
   a which   b whom   c –

2 The student ___ lent you his textbooks instead of selling them was extremely generous.
   a whom   b which   c who

3 Paula is only one of the many employees ___ they've made redundant.
   a whose   b when   c –

4 That's the factory ___ they make those cars you like so much.
   a where   b that   c when

5 Andrew and Linda, ___ children go to the same school as ours, are moving into the house next door.
   a which   b whose   c that

6 I'm afraid they've devalued our currency, ___ makes foreign holidays prohibitively expensive.
   a which   b when   c that

7 It wasn't until the following year ___ they were able to afford to buy a car.
   a which   b that   c where

8 We love going on holiday in May, ___ all the hills are covered in wild flowers.
   a when   b that   c –

C Match the first parts of the sentences 1–6 to the second parts a–f.

1 Dennis and Harriet are the couple ☐
2 1989 was the year ☐
3 Skiing is often best in March, ☐
4 I met your friend Adele, ☐
5 This is the village ☐
6 Now you know the reason ☐

a who lent us their cottage for the summer holidays.
b whose mother is organising the garage sale.
c why he didn't want to invest in the business.
d where my father was born.
e when the weather is good and there is plenty of snow.
f in which we started up the business.

D Rewrite the sentences using present, past or perfect participle clauses and the verbs given.

1 Before _____, please make sure you've tidied your room. (go out)
2 _____ half her salary for six months, Nadia decided to splash out on a holiday. (save)
3 _____ both calm and easy going, Terence never loses his temper. (be)
4 _____ a great deal of money, Alice was now able to pay all her debts. (inherit)
5 The goods _____ from the warehouse hadn't arrived. (order)
6 _____ the earthquake, the people now planned to rebuild the city. (survive)

E Complete the cleft sentences with these words.

| all   reason   thing   what   when   where |

1 _____ concerns us is the state of the economy.
2 _____ you have to do is put a little aside at the end of every month.
3 The _____ that really upset me was their lack of honesty.
4 The _____ I was so angry was because they hadn't told me the truth.
5 University is _____ you make your best friends.
6 He says the day he stops enjoying his job is _____ he'll retire.

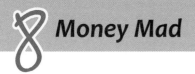

Listening

For questions 1–14, choose the best answer, a, b or c, that answers each question appropriately.

1 a It's all gone on bills, I'm afraid.
   b It's a good idea to save.
   c She spent a fortune on books last month.

2 a I've got enough cards.
   b Actually, I haven't got that many!
   c I never use credit cards.

3 a I can lend you some money.
   b OK, but he'll have to pay us back at the end of the month.
   c You haven't got a job at the moment.

4 a Actually, I should get one soon.
   b She got a pay rise last month.
   c They usually pay salaries on the first of the month.

5 a They're paying 500 euros a month.
   b She's asked for a huge loan to help meet her repayments.
   c Fortunately, I've paid the loan off with my redundancy money.

6 a I've made a 10% profit this year.
   b We've made a healthy profit on this transaction.
   c They've made a loss, unfortunately.

7 a Not at all, so long as I have them by the end of the day.
   b Yes, I have it in mind too.
   c I have a mind to do them tomorrow.

8 a She doesn't have the accounts.
   b I'm not sure, but I'd say she'll get them tomorrow or the next day.
   c She's expecting to do the accounts by the end of the year.

9 a We hope so, but we won't know for sure till the end of the month.
   b Yes, there are sales figures available for the first half of the year.
   c That's right, the sales figures were down last month.

10 a It's easy to buy shares.
    b Buying shares in blue chip companies is a sound investment.
    c They haven't done particularly well, but they haven't gone down.

11 a Investing in high tech companies could be profitable, but also risky.
    b This high tech company has given us our best return.
    c The highest return is often the riskiest investment.

12 a You have no duty to pay for gifts.
    b All gifts are duty free.
    c No, you don't, unless their value exceeds £40.

13 a Yes, I do, which is why I've decided to get out of it.
    b Yes, I do, which is why I'm going to invest in it.
    c No, I don't, which is why I won't be investing in it.

14 a Yes, you can get dollars at the bank.
    b I think you'll get a better rate if you book your currency online.
    c I'm pretty sure you'll get a poor rate of exchange at the airport.

Writing

A Read the writing task below and answer the questions.

You read the following announcement in a college magazine.

> *Online auction websites like eBay are more popular than ever. We would like you, the readers, to submit articles telling us what you like and dislike about online auction websites, and explain how you think they affect conventional shops.*
>
> *We will publish the most interesting articles.*

1 Who will be reading your article?
2 What register will you use?
3 What will you be writing about?

B Read the model article and summarise the three main paragraphs.

The good and bad of online auction websites

Online auction websites like eBay have been changing the way we buy and sell goods since the mid 1990s. Because they are so convenient, people often use them instead of going to the shops. But are online auction websites safe and how are they affecting the retail industry?

The ease with which goods can be bought and sold, has made auction websites very popular. Also, they have become the obvious destination for people wanting to sell items due to the sheer quantity of people visiting them. A major benefit is their simplicity: you just take a photo, upload it and wait for someone to make you the best offer for your goods.

Although auction websites sound ideal, there have been cases of fraud. For example, you've paid for the goods and they never arrive or are damaged. Another possible disadvantage includes the time-consuming business of taking photos, adding descriptions and shipping items off once they've been bought.

But how are online auctions affecting the shops in our towns and cities? Well, it's conceivable that you could do all your buying and selling on eBay and never set foot in a shop. This is great for the individual but not so great for the retail industry. There is little doubt that shops have been closing as a result.

Although there are drawbacks to auction websites, it seems that these are outweighed by their advantages and people will carry on using them despite their effect on conventional shops. Only the strongest will survive.

C Read and complete the writing task below.

You read the following announcement in a college magazine.

> *Large supermarkets and hypermarkets are more popular than ever. We would like you, the readers, to submit articles telling us what you like and dislike about such places, and explain how you think they affect small shops and farmer's markets.*
>
> *We will publish the most interesting articles.*

*Write your **article** in 220–260 words in an appropriate style.*

Watch the clock!

Spend 5 minutes reading the task and planning your article.

Spend 30 minutes writing your article.

Spend 5 minutes checking and editing your article.

Remember!

When writing an article, your main aim is to attract the reader's attention and give them your views on a topic. Make sure you use the right register. Organise your article into paragraphs and use topic sentences as well as expressions that help engage the reader. See the Writing Reference for articles on page 182 of the Student's Book for further help.

Vocabulary

A Choose the correct answers.

1 You'd never guess she has a(n) ___ leg.
a pretend
b artificial
c fake
d reproduction

2 Machines have replaced many ___ labourers.
a physical
b actual
c manual
d handy

3 Most metals are good ___ of heat.
a components
b compositions
c conducts
d conductors

4 All surgical instruments must be ___ after use.
a sterilised
b sanitised
c laundered
d vacuumed

5 One of the ___ of gold is that it doesn't rust.
a properties
b conditions
c elements
d constraints

6 There was a(n) ___ in the results, so they tested again.
a disagreement
b distinction
c anomaly
d source

7 I replaced my inkjet printer with a ___ printer.
a control
b laser
c memory
d hard

8 We provide cutting ___ technology in alarm systems.
a side
b edge
c angle
d rim

9 All my photos are here, on my ___ stick.
a recall
b recollection
c memory
d message

10 Look, it's not ___ science. Anyone can learn to do it.
a space
b hard
c complex
d rocket

11 There aren't many 500 euro notes in ___.
a circulation
b motion
c flow
d movement

12 Unfortunately, she was paid with ___ notes.
a inauthentic
b valueless
c false
d counterfeit

13 He's in a lot of debt. He ___ thousands of euros.
a owns
b earns
c owes
d clears

14 What's the ___ in Poland? Is it the euro?
a coin
b currency
c denomination
d exchange

15 She bought a lot of ___ in renewable energy companies.
a commodities
b shares
c assets
d investments

16 Let's all ___ in and buy something for Jim's birthday.
a chip
b chop
c fork
d splash

17 Have you put ___ a deposit on the house you're buying?
a up
b in
c over
d down

18 We didn't make a profit; we made a ___.
a fortune
b balance
c loss
d debt

19 I receive a bank ___ every month.
a account
b balance
c document
d statement

20 There's a ___ market in the square on Sunday.
a fly
b flea
c stock
d stack

Grammar

B **Choose the correct answers.**

1 As long as you ___ to work, you'll do very well.
   a prepare
   b prepared
   c are prepared
   d had been prepared

2 ___ your help, I wouldn't have managed to find it.
   a Supposing
   b But for
   c Provided
   d Unless

3 If you ___ blue and yellow, you get green.
   a mix
   b will mix
   c mixed
   d had mixed

4 I ___ if you hadn't arrived then.
   a will leave
   b will have left
   c would leave
   d would have left

5 They ___ in unless they are accompanied by an adult.
   a won't be allowed
   b wouldn't be allowed
   c wouldn't have been allowed
   d weren't allowed

6 I don't know what ___ if you hadn't arrived then.
   a will happen
   b would happen
   c would have happened
   d would have been happening

7 I wouldn't have got the card if you ___ it early.
   a don't post
   b didn't post
   c hadn't posted
   d hadn't been posting

8 ___ had Sue left for work than her boss rang.
   a No sooner
   b As soon
   c Only
   d Not only

9 If only I ___ more for the exam!
   a will revise
   b would revise
   c had revised
   d would have revised

10 ___ had we been so moved by a film.
   a Not only
   b Rarely
   c Little
   d Only

11 That's the couple ___ children I used to look after.
   a which
   b of which
   c who
   d whose

12 That's the house ___ I was born.
   a -
   b which
   c that
   d where

13 Pamela, ___ married to Robert, is my first cousin.
   a that
   b whose
   c who's
   d which

14 I'm really enjoying the book ___ I'm reading.
   a -
   b what
   c whose
   d where

15 ___ coat is this? It's not yours, is it?
   a Which
   b What
   c Who
   d Whose

16 Properly ___, it should last you a lifetime.
   a looking after
   b after looking
   c looked after
   d after looked

17 The thing ___ me most about it is his dishonesty.
   a what bothers
   b that bothers
   c bothers
   d would bother

18 ___ in France, she speaks fluent French.
   a Educating
   b Education
   c Having educated
   d Having been educated

19 ___ my message cancelling the meeting, he waited.
   a Received
   b Not received
   c Not having received
   d Having received

20 ___ do best are the ones who train the hardest.
   a The athletes who
   b Whom
   c Which athletes
   d What athletes

Use of English

C Complete the text by writing one word in each gap.

The invention of the microwave oven

We wouldn't have microwave ovens today but **(1)** _____ an accidental discovery made by Percy Spencer. Spencer was an American engineer **(2)** _____ was working on radar technology in the 1940s. He was experimenting with microwaves one day, and **(3)** _____ sooner had he completed the experiment **(4)** _____ he realised a chocolate bar in his pocket **(5)** _____ melted. Supposing he knew the outcome beforehand, he **(6)** _____ not have had the chocolate bar in his pocket. **(7)** _____ discovered the effect, he tried to repeat the process on popcorn, thinking it would pop. As it turns out, he was spot **(8)** _____ – the experiment was a success. His third attempt was with an egg, **(9)** _____ ended up exploding in his face. **(10)** _____ the thoughtful engineer that he was, he decided to make a metal box – the first real 'oven' – to experiment using a controlled environment. Only **(11)** _____ did he know the microwaves were heating the food. Spencer decided to get his money's **(12)** _____ on the invention, and 1945 was the year **(13)** _____ he took out a patent. The cutting **(14)** _____ technology was first used publicly in 1947, when a company splashed **(15)** _____ on a machine that dispensed hot dogs in New York City's Grand Central Terminal.

D Complete the text with the correct form of the words.

The wealthiest of the wealthy

Every year, Forbes magazine puts out its famous list of **(1)** _____. The list provides people with an inside look at how much money the world's most **(2)** _____ people possess. Names such as computer software giant Bill Gates and Mexican businessman Carlos Slim, an investor and stock **(3)** _____, seem to appear at the top of the list year after year. The list is important because it is a(n) **(4)** _____ indicator of global wealth. For example, in 2008, when the world was suffering from a devastating **(5)** _____ crisis, these wealthiest people did in fact 'suffer'. In 2009's list, there was a net **(6)** _____ in the number of people on the list, the first time the list had seen such a **(7)** _____ in five years. Since then, the very rich have seen the value of their assets rise again as **(8)** _____ markets have generally improved. So what does the wealthiest person's bank **(9)** _____ look like? This man, the aforementioned Carlos Slim, has assets worth US$73 billion. We don't know what he actually has in **(10)** _____, but you can be assured it's probably a lot!

BILLION

PROSPER

TRADE
LEAD
ECONOMY
LOSE
GRADE
FINANCE
STATE

SAVE

E Think of one word only that can be used appropriately in all three sentences.

1   Isn't there a more _____ way to back up your files than burning them onto a CD?

The company decided to upgrade its operational systems to be more cost _____.

_____ immediately, all work injuries must be reported to the production line supervisor.

2   The stereo isn't working because one of the _____ in the back is broken.

Every month, Michael _____ money to his parents who live abroad.

I was supposed to see Debra at ten, but our _____ got crossed and we didn't meet.

3   This weekend's fundraiser was easy _____ – we raised over 2,000 euros in one afternoon!

Her family comes from old _____, as her great-grandfather was a wealthy inventor.

I don't earn a lot from giving maths lessons – it's just enough to give me pocket _____.

4   A company recently created the world's smallest computer _____.

Can you _____ in a little bit of cash for a birthday gift for Dawn?

The young inventor was just like his father – a _____ off the old block.

5   A _____ of experts decided that the product was not worth releasing on to the market.

There's a large _____ covering the access to the building's air vents.

You can adjust or remove programs from the computer by using the control _____.

F Complete the second sentences so that they have a similar meaning to the first sentences using the words in bold. Use between three and six words.

1   The genius inventor had ideas that were far more advanced than his peers.

LIGHT

The genius inventor's ideas were _____ his peers.

2   You should be able to solve the problem as it isn't terribly difficult to understand.

ROCKET

You should be able to solve the problem as _____.

3   My friend Maria spends cash like she has a lot of it, but she will soon be broke.

THROWS

My friend Maria, _____ like she's rich, will soon be broke.

4   He is wealthy because he's really good with money.

REASON

The _____ he's really good with money.

5   The country's first bank was set up in 1883.

YEAR

_____ the country's first bank was set up.

6   Nathan sold the chair to John for what he paid for it.

COST

Nathan sold the chair to John _____.

7   When Paul encounters a problem at work, he often overreacts.

BUTTON

Paul tends to _____ when he comes across a problem at work.

8   You would have finished on time if you didn't try to do what had already been done.

HAD

If only you _____ the wheel, you would have finished on time.

9 All That Jazz!

Reading

Read the texts and answer the questions.

A

Cuban music is born from the rich amalgamation of Spanish folk music formulas and African rhythms. The phenomenal richness of Spanish folklore, mixed with the vigour of African music, created an explosive and exuberant musical tapestry. **Quinteto Cha** is composed of musicians of different nationalities who play their own interpretations of traditional Cuban music. Mexican singer and songwriter Luis Angulo is backed by four Europeans: female bassist Irmgard Lerch, Alex Xanthis on percussion, flautist Henry Eberhard and guitarist Günter Kleinmann.

B

The sheep-herding mountaineers of Poland used a style of singing called *bialy glos* or 'white voice'; a type of powerful, melodic screaming used to communicate across long distances. **Warsaw Village Ban** travelled Poland's countryside in search of the old people who could recall the traditional folk music of their regions. The band combines traditional music and experiments with modern instrumentation and subject matter. The Warsaw Village Band's youthful but mature take on Poland's roots music has allowed them to introduce this tradition to audiences around the world.

C

The multi-talented Brazilian artist known simply as **Joyce** combines song-writing, guitar-playing, vocal skills and a flair for feminist themes in her lyrics in a way that makes her unique. On her debut album *Astronauta – Songs of Elis*, Joyce lends her sunny, jazz-savvy voice and guitar work to a programme of beloved Brazilian classics recorded in the '60s and '70s by the late Elis Regina, the revered vocalist. *Astronauta* features a cast of Brazilian and North American jazz musicians of global renown. The talents of Grammy award-winning tenor saxophonist Joe Lovano and pianists Mulgrew Miller and Renee Rosnes meld effortlessly with Joyce's voice and guitar.

D

Cherish the Ladies is an all-female Irish traditional group based in the United States, which first came together in 1985 to perform at a one-off concept concert. Led by native New Yorker Joanie Madden – a former All-Ireland tin whistle champ – Cherish the Ladies has evolved into one of the most influential and beloved traditional Irish music acts on either side of the Atlantic. The Ladies' ever-changing roster has included some of the most impressive women in Irish traditional music, from all over the Irish diaspora – including Cathie Ryan, Aoife Clancy, Liz Knowles, and Marie Reilly.

E

Born in the village of Mazoso, in the province of Benguela, Angola, **Moises and Jose Kafala** both rose to national fame individually before their debut performance together in 1987 in Luanda. The Kafala's music is best described as Angolan folk music. Their songs reflect real-life experiences, while painting poetic portraits of Angola's 30-year-long war and continued struggle for national reconciliation. Using a single guitar and a flute, the Kafalas are able to tell stories of war, sadness, love and joy with conviction and heartbreaking vocal harmonies which have been known to provoke uncontrollable tears to well up in the eyes of those listening.

F

Despite his thin, sometimes strained voice, **Gregory Isaacs** is one of reggae's all-time greatest singers, a master of subtle phrasing and sly innuendo who has voiced some of the music's best-known hits. A prolific recording artist and performer, Isaacs has penned classic roots anthems, as well as truly sappy lover's rock. But no matter which side of Isaacs manifests itself on stage, he's a rivetting performer, driving crowds into a frenzy with the smallest of gestures. For this he's been dubbed 'The Cool Ruler' and is one of the best-loved performers of Jamaican audiences, who have stuck loyally by the singer even when his turbulent personal life got in the way of the music.

Read the texts and find the following information. In which section are the following mentioned?

a performer who sings, writes songs and plays an instrument	1	☐
a single-sex group of musicians that is not fixed	2	☐
an international musical quintet	3	☐
musicians based in one country playing music from another	4	☐
a fusion of traditional and experimental music	5	☐
a popular musician who has performed in many concerts	6	☐
a fusion of two ethnic musical traditions	7	☐
music with biographical themes set in troubled times	8	☐
a group that has performed internationally	9	☐
musicians who were famous individually before joining forces	10	☐
a musician who embraces two distinct musical traditions	11	☐
an artist who has just brought out their first album	12	☐

Vocabulary

A Choose the correct answers.

1 There are sites where you can get free music ___ on the Internet, but you need to know where to look.
   a loadings   b downloads   c copies

2 I love that song and if you listen to the ___, you'll realise it's incredibly sad.
   a poetry   b sounds   c lyrics

3 The artist would ___ his subject from many different angles before deciding on a final pose.
   a sketch   b doodle   c copy

4 In three days, they've sold over 5,000 ___ of their new single! It's fantastic news.
   a albums   b numbers   c copies

5 If you want to be a classical musician, you are going to have to learn how to ___ music.
   a decipher   b read   c listen

6 The official music ___ in the UK include classical as well as popular music.
   a lists   b tables   c charts

7 ___ painting, which involves painting on wet plaster, is quite rare these days, compared to the Renaissance.
   a Free   b Fresh   c Fresco

8 Her favourite painting is a ___ of a bowl of fruit by Gauguin. You can see it at the National Gallery in London.
   a still life   b portrait   c life drawing

B Complete the text with these words.

canvas   commissions   controversy   landscapes   movement   oil   portrait   subjects

Oskar Kokoschka

Oskar Kokoschka was a major figure of the Expressionist **(1)** _____.
He was born in Austria in 1886 and died in Switzerland aged 93. His first paintings
and plays caused so much **(2)** _____ that he was dismissed from
the Vienna School of Arts and Crafts in 1909. Around the same time, he became
friends with architect Adolf Loos, whose **(3)** _____ he painted,
and who helped him get his first **(4)** _____. Kokoschka not only
painted portraits, he also painted many **(5)** _____ as well as writing
plays and poetry. *The Bride of the Wind* is probably his most famous painting. It
is a(n) **(6)** _____ painting on **(7)** _____ and depicts the
painter with the love of his life, Alma Mahler, widow of composer Gustav Mahler.
Other **(8)** _____ included actors, politicians and socialites of the time.

69

C Complete the sentences with the correct form of the words.

1 These are lovely _____ of the original paintings, but I do wish I could afford to buy an original. REPRODUCE

2 Picasso's first _____ in Paris in 1901 was a critical failure, which is ironic considering how famous and successful he became. EXHIBIT

3 The Sistine Chapel ceiling is considered by many to be the _____ of Michelangelo's life's work. CULMINATE

4 Did you see Meryl Streep in *The Iron Lady*? I think it was her best _____ to date. PERFORM

5 After rehearsing for so long, the actors were ready for the _____ night of their new play. OPEN

6 Bob Dylan's second wife, Carolyn Dennis, was one of his long-term _____ singers. BACK

D Circle the correct words.

1 He used to play avant-garde music, but now he's basically a(n) mainstream / alternative musician.

2 He's a typical musician, never at home, always on road / tour.

3 We thought we'd see her sculptures in the gallery, but they weren't on display / parade.

4 Adele's debut / opening album, *19*, was a massive success.

5 She's been under agreement / contract to the record label XL Recordings since 2006.

6 Who is the lead solo / vocalist for the band Kasabian? Is it Tom Meighan?

7 I'm reciting a poem at school tomorrow and I have to learn it by chest / heart.

8 Whose authority / management were the group under when they became famous?

E Match the phrases or sentences 1–8 to the phrases or sentences a–h.

1 She's the opposite of modest and ☐

2 If you make such a song and dance about a little test, ☐

3 That's not what you said before, so ☐

4 We're going to have to face ☐

5 Nobody wanted the old amplifier ☐

6 He told me my painting was wonderful, which ☐

7 When the police brought him in, ☐

8 Elly loves your piano playing and ☐

a the music sooner or later.

b he just sang like a canary and confessed everything.

c how will you cope with your final exams?

d she has been singing your praises.

e she's always blowing her own trumpet.

f was music to my ears!

g what made you change your tune?

h so I was able to buy it for a song.

Grammar

A Tick the correct sentences. Correct the sentences that are wrong.

1 I don't think Lady Gaga is a most talented singer than Katy Perry, do you? ☐

2 Daniel Radcliffe is one of the best-known actors in the world. ☐

3 The Russian *War and Peace* is among the longest films ever made. ☐

4 Mary felt she wasn't such gifted a musician as her sister. ☐

5 Those paintings aren't as impressive so you'd imagine. ☐

6 He's performed in twice as many films as plays. ☐

7 They're not so expensive tickets as I'd thought they'd be. ☐

8 It's as brilliant a performance as you'll ever see in your life. ☐

B Complete the second sentences so that they have a similar meaning to the first sentences. Use the words in bold.

1 I hadn't expected his performance to be so bad. **much**
   His performance was _____ I had expected.

2 She isn't quite as tall in real life as she appears to be in her films. **bit**
   In real life she is _____ she appears to be in her films.

3 There were nowhere near as many as fifty people at the concert. **considerably**
   There were _____ fifty people at the concert.

4 They're certainly not as popular as they used to be. **deal**
   They're _____ they used to be.

5 He is nice, but his sister the artist is much more interesting. **lot**
   He is _____ his sister the artist.

6 The music festival had only five bands last year, but there were 30 this year. **far**
   This year there were _____ last year at the music festival.

C Complete the text with the correct form of the words in brackets.

The Edinburgh Festival

The Edinburgh Festival, which takes place in August every year, is
(1) _____ (important) cultural event in
Scotland and one of **(2)** _____ (large)
and **(3)** _____ (well known) in Europe,
if not the world. It is **(4)** _____
(vibrant) and original as it was when I first visited twenty years ago, but
there is no doubt that the **(5)** _____
(long) it goes on and the **(6)** _____
(big) it gets, the **(7)** _____ (sprawling)
it becomes. Nowadays, there are venues all over Edinburgh, not only
in the city centre. Audiences discover a massive range of cultural
experiences and some of **(8)** _____
(entertaining) performers in the world. Not only can you see
established artists in the main festival, but you can also experience
the Edinburgh Festival Fringe, which runs in parallel and is probably
(9) _____ (visited) of its type in
the world. Anybody can put on a show at the Fringe, from theatre
students to individuals who just want to have a go. In fact, many of our
(10) _____ (well loved) actors and
comedians started out at the Fringe, performing in small venues to a
handful of spectators, more often than not, free of charge.

D Complete the sentences with the words in brackets and *too* or *enough*.

1 The critics said she wasn't _____ (serious) for the role.

2 To be honest, I'm much _____ (tired) to go out to the theatre tonight.

3 They were asked to leave the library because they weren't talking _____ (quietly).

4 Do you think he's _____ (talented) to get into the local school for the performing arts?

5 I'm afraid Simon is much _____ (lazy) to practise the piano every day.

6 Do you think it's _____ (late) for me to take up an instrument?

7 He hadn't produced _____ (paintings) to put on an exhibition.

8 Unfortunately, he's become _____ (famous) to go out unrecognised.

E Complete the sentences with these words and *so* or *such*.

| complex   determination   easy   flop   long   positive |

1 There was _____ a _____ response to the exhibition that they kept it open for another month.

2 The play was _____ a _____ that it closed after a fortnight.

3 The concert was _____ _____ that some people started leaving before the end.

4 _____ _____ was his symphony as to make it almost impossible to find musicians to play it.

5 It was _____ _____ a piece that he learnt how to play it in a morning.

6 _____ was her _____ to go to drama school that she was prepared to apply for a place three times.

Listening

You will hear two people talking about the Damien Hirst exhibition at the Tate Modern in London. For questions 1–6, choose the best answer, a, b, c or d.

1 What does the woman think of the Hirst exhibition at the Tate Modern?
   a She was very impressed.
   b She wonders if it should have been put on at all.
   c She hated it.
   d She thought it was very courageous.

2 What do the man and woman agree about?
   a Hirst's works aren't beautiful.
   b Hirst's works are moving.
   c Hirst is a conceptual artist.
   d Hirst's works are fragile.

3 He thinks the work entitled *In and Out of Love* is brilliant because
   a it's beautiful.
   b it's thought provoking.
   c it captures what love is.
   d it creates controversy.

4 The man thinks the butterfly room isn't cruel because the butterflies
   a were provided with everything they needed.
   b could fly around freely.
   c were safe from predators in the museum.
   d didn't feel any pain.

5 Why does the woman think Hirst isn't a great artist?
   a His ideas aren't original.
   b His diamond skull costs too much.
   c He's very rich.
   d He doesn't make his own pieces.

6 What is the purpose of *memento mori* objects?
   a They represent the spirit of our times.
   b They remind us that our lives will end one day.
   c They are to be admired for their beauty.
   d They create a historical context.

Writing

A Read the writing task below and write T (true) or F (false).

You see the following announcement in an international art magazine.

> **Do you go to art exhibitions?**
>
> *We are conducting a survey comparing art exhibitions around the world. We would like you, our readers, to write a report about an art exhibition you've been to. In your report you should:*
>
> - *introduce the exhibition*
> - *describe what you liked about the exhibition*
> - *describe any problems you experienced*
> - *suggest improvements that you would like to see*

1 Your target readers aren't interested in art.

2 You should write in a chatty, very informal style.

3 You should give your opinion and make suggestions.

4 You shouldn't mention any living artists.

Write your report.

B Read the model article and complete it with these words in the correct form.

art   attend   improve   privilege   simple

The Kerry Mallin exhibition at MOMA

I was **(1)** _____ to attend the Kerry Mallin exhibition at MOMA (The Museum of Modern Art) last week. It is a stunning show, which has already drawn a record number of visitors.

(2) _____, Kerry Mallin has matured and developed in a way that could not have been predicted. Out are the landscapes we had become accustomed to and in are exquisite portraits in pastels, reminiscent of the formal portraits of the 18th century, with a(n) **(3)** _____ that is breathtakingly beautiful. The public and critics alike have been enthralled and there have been queues outside the museum all this week.

There is room for **(4)** _____, however, in the way the paintings are displayed. One wall is dedicated to Mallin's portraits of the homeless and is covered in so many works that is becomes difficult to take them all in. I fear those that aren't at eye level do not receive the **(5)** _____ they deserve, which is a very great shame, as they are not only moving but beautifully composed.

I would therefore recommend that either fewer works are displayed or another wall is used to hang some of the crowded paintings. I would also suggest that MOMA remain open for an extra hour per day to allow more visitors to enjoy the wonders of Kerry Mallin's works.

C Read and complete the writing task below.

You read the following announcement in a college art magazine.

> **Do you go to museums?**
>
> *We are conducting a survey comparing museums around the world. We would like you, our readers, to write a report about a museum you've been to. In your report you should:*
>
> - *introduce the museum*
> - *outline your favourite part of the museum*
> - *describe any problems you experienced*
> - *suggest improvements that you would like to see.*

Write your **report** in 220–260 words in an appropriate style.

Remember!

When writing a report, your main aim is to provide factual information and to give your opinion on how something could be improved. Organise your report into paragraphs and use the appropriate style according to your readers. See the Writing Reference for reports on page 183 of the Student's Book for further help.

watch the clock!

 Spend 5 minutes reading the task and planning your report.

 Spend 30 minutes writing your report.

 Spend 5 minutes checking and editing your report.

10 Modern Living

Reading

Read the article and choose the answer (a, b, c or d) which fits best according to the text.

Bikes and buses propel Mexico City to prize in sustainable transport

Bicycles, pedestrian-friendly plazas and walkways, new bus lines, and parking meters are combining to transform parts of Mexico City from a traffic nightmare to a commuter's paradise. The Mexican capital, one of the world's most populated urban areas, has captured this year's Sustainable Transport Award, the Institute for Transportation and Development Policy (ITDP) has announced.

As recently as late 2011, Mexico City commuters reported enduring the most painful commute among respondents to an IBM survey. Based on factors such as roadway traffic, stress levels, and commute times, the city scored worse than 19 other cities, including Beijing, China, and Nairobi, Kenya. Mexico City has seen its roadways swell beyond capacity to more than four million vehicles, which are owned, increasingly, by a growing middle class.

But the city has also made strides to reorient itself around public spaces and people, rather than cars and driving. 'They really changed quite fundamentally the direction and vision of the city, and a lot of it was in 2012,' said Walter Hook, Chief Executive of ITDP, an international non-profit organisation that works with cities to reduce greenhouse gas emissions and improve the quality of urban life.

Since 2011, Mexico City has added two new bus corridors to its Metrobus system, connecting the narrow streets in the historic centre to the airport and making it the longest bus rapid transit (BRT) system in Latin America. The city also added nearly 90 stations and 1,200 new bicycles to the Ecobici bike-sharing programme. It began to reform on-street parking, it improved pavements, and it also established new walkways.

The day-to-day experience of getting around the city centre has changed dramatically. Two years ago, Hook said in an interview, 'If you tried to get across the historical core of Mexico City, you couldn't take a bus or a taxi or anything that would travel more than three miles an hour. It was virtually at a standstill.' Most likely, he said, you would ride in an old minibus run by an unregulated operator, or drive a car. And the narrow streets of the historic city centre – a UNESCO World Heritage site – would be crowded with street vendors, trash, and illegally parked vehicles, he said. 'Now you'd be on a beautiful street, in an ultramodern bus – very clean, absolutely safe.'

Not all of the changes in Mexico City have received a universally warm welcome. The new parking system, called ecoParq, introduced multispace meters to thousands of parking spots on streets where parking previously had been free – officially free, anyway. In reality, much on-street parking was controlled by unregulated valets or attendants known as *franeleros*, who would stake out territories and charge drivers small fees to park and receive protection in their spaces. When the city hired a contractor to take over parking management, starting in the upscale *Polanco* district, *franeleros* protested. They reportedly marched through the neighbourhood carrying signs bearing messages such as, 'The streets are not for sale,' and 'A parking meter doesn't take care of your car.'

Mexico City's efforts are part of much larger shifts taking place internationally. 'Sustainable transport systems go hand in hand with low emissions development and livable cities,' remarked Sophie Punte, Executive Director of Clear Air Asia, in a statement. 'Mexico City's success has proven that developing cities can achieve this, and we expect many Asian cities to follow suit.'

The pool of cities moving towards more sustainable transport systems is only growing, said Hook. 'Each year we're finding more and more cities that have made fairly dramatic changes to really retake the city,' Hook said. 'Cities are looking at their mass transit investments now not only as a way of getting people from point A to point B, but also as a way of revitalizing strategic locations and bringing parts of the city back to life.'

1 At the end of 2011, people in Mexico City
  a were enjoying an improved transport system.
  b were still parking free of charge in the city centre.
  c were more stressed than commuters in some other cities.
  d owned more cars than the middle-classes in Beijing and Nairobi.

2 The ITDP
  a has given Mexico City a number of awards.
  b conducts surveys for IBM.
  c advises cities on environmentally-friendly practices.
  d creates public spaces for people.

3 Improvements to the transport system include
  a more bus routes and a new parking system.
  b free parking and pedestrianised streets.
  c wider roads and bicycle lanes.
  d new pavements and cleaner streets.

4 Transport in Mexico City used to be dominated by
  a privately-owned vehicles.
  b buses and cyclists.
  c unregulated parking valets known as *franeleros*.
  d pedestrians and public transport.

5 *Franeleros* are unhappy about the new parking system because
  a they think parking should be free of charge.
  b ecoParq is too expensive.
  c it can take care of people's cars.
  d it has destroyed their livelihoods.

6 Mexico City's success in improving its transport system
  a is unlikely to be sustainable.
  b proves that people can get from point A to point B easily.
  c is likely to inspire other cities to do the same.
  d couldn't have been done before now.

Vocabulary

A Complete the words in the sentences.

1 Paris, London and New York are lively, c _ _ _ _ _ _ _ _ _ _ cities with multi-ethnic populations.

2 Emily's injuries mean she's had to lead a much more s _ _ _ _ _ _ _ life than she used to and has therefore put on a lot of weight.

3 Paul's f _ _ _ _ _ _ _ years were spent in the country so it is no wonder that he has decided to leave the city for village life.

4 Pilots undergo r _ _ _ _ _ _ _ training before they are allowed to fly commercial planes.

5 I'm reading a book about p _ _ _ _ _ _ _ _ life in the 19ᵗʰ century. It's set in a small town 100 kilometres from London.

6 I think this table is a bit p _ _ _ _ _ for us. We can't really afford it.

7 He never socialises, preferring to lead a quiet, s _ _ _ _ _ _ _ life.

8 My life is so h _ _ _ _ _ at the moment, I haven't got time for any leisure activities at all.

B Complete the text with these words in the correct form.

balance   concern   endure   excel   juggle   outdo   spoil   struggle

Life as a single parent

Few people would choose to bring up their children on their own. However, there are two million single parents in Britain today – just over a quarter of all households with dependent children. But who are these parents **(1)** _____ to raise their children alone?

The average single parent is female, close to forty, and divorced. Contrary to what many would have us believe, over half of the UK's single parents aren't unemployed. They are **(2)** _____ work and child rearing. Many are also **(3)** _____ a life of poverty compared to parents with partners. It is no wonder, then, that life for typical single mother Maria Barton is a(n) **(4)** _____ act between work and childcare. Maria is **(5)** _____ about her children's welfare and future. There is little chance of her **(6)** _____ her children – on the contrary, by the time they started school, both Josh and Ruby had taken on responsibilities their cousins had yet to master at college: making their own breakfast, keeping their rooms tidy and helping out with housework. Maria was determined not to be a statistic – a single mother living in poverty. She has **(7)** _____ at her job, has been promoted every couple of years and has now **(8)** _____ all her married friends in terms of salary and the home she can afford for herself and her children.

C The words in bold are in the wrong sentences. Write each word next to the correct sentence.

1 The city of São Paulo in Brazil is one of the most densely populated **sociable** areas in the world. _____

2 **Irritable** exercising is almost as harmful as never doing any exercise at all and can damage the body. _____

3 Participation in school sports is a possible factor in leading a more **addictive** lifestyle in adult life. _____

4 Going on such a strict diet has made Sonia particularly **obsessive** at the moment. She keeps losing her temper! _____

5 People who are **active** to chest infections should not live in places with high levels of atmospheric pollution. _____

6 You know coffee is **susceptible**, don't you? You're bound to get a headache if you stop drinking it from one day to the next. _____

7 Before she became a famous actress, she claims she was a naïve and **metropolitan** girl. _____

8 You're always out and about with your friends. I think you're the most **unsophisticated** person I know! _____

D Match the words 1–8 with the words a–h.

1 come up ☐
2 safe and ☐
3 ruin ☐
4 burn the candle ☐
5 do ☐
6 wear ☐
7 throw in ☐
8 hit ☐

a without
b your chances
c against
d rock bottom
e sound
f the towel
g at both ends
h down

E Complete the sentences with an expression from exercise D in the correct form.

1 Things can't get any worse now that he has _____. From now on the only way is up.

2 They _____ a set of problems which seemed quite insurmountable.

3 It's such a relief to have the children home, _____ after their ordeal.

4 I'm not surprised you're exhausted. That's what happens if you _____.

5 After such an angry outburst at work, I'm afraid you've _____ of getting a promotion.

6 Working long hours in such awful conditions will eventually _____ even the strongest person.

7 It's no use. I can't do this job – I've tried for long enough. I'm _____.

8 You'll have to _____ milk in your tea this morning. There's none in the fridge.

Grammar

A Circle the correct words in the text.

Not getting the promotion you deserve?

You love your job and you've been doing it to the best of your ability for years. But as time goes by, your job description remains the same. Why **(1)** are you overlooking / are you being overlooked? Why **(2)** aren't you being promoted / aren't you promoting? You say you keep your head down and get on with the job. Is that perhaps why **(3)** you've not chosen / you haven't been chosen? Are you blending in too much and simply **(4)** not being noticed / not noticing? Employers want to see staff **(5)** dealing with / being dealt with work efficiently and without fuss. In order to attain your much-longed-for promotion you need **(6)** to see / to be seen to be doing just that. Obviously, you need **(7)** to be delivered / to deliver your work on time. You must also ensure it is of the highest quality and that this **(8)** is recognised / has recognised by your boss as well as your colleagues. You don't want to boast, you just want to make sure you **(9)** are identified / should be identified as an efficient and talented member of the team. You want to be appreciated. But remember Rome **(10)** didn't build / wasn't built in a day, so you'll probably need to be patient.

B Rewrite the sentences using passive constructions.

1 I don't think they gave the award to the most deserving person.
   I don't think the award _____.

2 People know there aren't any more opportunities for growth this year.
   It _____.

3 The factory workers expect redundancies to be made.
   Redundancies _____.

4 Somebody has eaten all the biscuits I got for the meeting.
   All the biscuits _____.

5 They decided that our groups would be merged.
   It _____.

6 They expect the schools to close early.
   The _____.

C Complete the sentences with the words in brackets in the correct form.

1 Helen _____ (appear / lose) her glasses. She can't find them anywhere.

2 She's not getting better, you know. In fact, she _____ (seem / get) worse.

3 They _____ (appear / leave) the country for good and their house has been sold.

4 Laurence _____ (seems / be) very relaxed despite having an interview this afternoon.

5 It's been a slow process, but the traffic _____ (appear / improve) at last.

6 My phone _____ (seem / disappear). Have you seen it anywhere?

D Complete the sentences with these verbs in the correct form.

break   clean   decorate   dye   paint   remove   ruin   stick

1 They're having the house _____ a lovely yellow before their daughter's wedding.

2 We're having our living room _____ by an interior designer.

3 She got her silk dress _____ in the car door and now it's ruined.

4 Nancy has had her hair _____ pink. It looks fantastic!

5 We had all our furniture _____ before the builders came. It's all in storage now.

6 My sat nav was stolen when I had my car _____ into last week.

7 Did you get the windows _____ professionally or did you do them yourself?

8 Be careful eating on the sofa; I don't want it _____ when you spill your dinner on it.

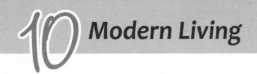

E **Complete the second sentences so that they have the same meaning as the first sentences.**

1 It appears that there might have been a misunderstanding. I'm sure we can resolve the problem.

There _____ a misunderstanding. I'm sure the problem

_____ .

2 It seems as if they've adapted to their new circumstances very well. They appear to be quite settled and happy.

They _____ to their new circumstances very well. It appears

_____ quite settled and happy.

3 It doesn't seem as if she's listened to a word you said. She doesn't seem to have followed any of your advice.

She _____ a word you said. It doesn't _____ any of your advice.

4 It appears that you didn't really mean it when you offered to help. I'm asking you now and you don't seem very keen to lend a hand.

You don't _____ when you offered to help. I'm asking you now and it doesn't

_____ to lend a hand.

5 It seems that you have forgotten your promise to lend me the book. I see that Monica is reading it now.

You _____ to lend me the book. Monica seems _____ now.

6 It appears that nobody has done the washing up. Every dish in the house seems to have been used.

Nobody _____ the washing-up. It _____ .

Listening

You will hear five people talking about their lifestyles. Complete both tasks as you listen.

Task 1

For questions 1–5, choose from the list A–H the reason which best reflects why each person chose his or her current lifestyle.

1 Speaker 1 ☐
2 Speaker 2 ☐
3 Speaker 3 ☐
4 Speaker 4 ☐
5 Speaker 5 ☐

A wanting a better paid job
B being unemployed
C following a family tradition
D a change in his/her personal life
E disillusionment with his/her first job
F being confident about a career choice
G knowing when to ask for a promotion
H not having time to enjoy what he/she worked for

Task 2

For questions 6–10, choose from the list A–H the main advantage of the lifestyle mentioned by each speaker.

6 Speaker 1 ☐
7 Speaker 2 ☐
8 Speaker 3 ☐
9 Speaker 4 ☐
10 Speaker 5 ☐

A good future prospects
B enjoying a high-flying job
C running his/her own business
D feeling pride in his/her job
E working for a good employer
F spending more time with family
G learning on the job
H living in a larger property

Writing

A Read the writing task below and write T (true) or F (false) or DK (don't know).

You read the following announcement in an international magazine.

> ### *The plusses and minuses of country living*
>
> *Town and Country magazine invites its readers to give their views on living in the country in the 21*st *century. What are the advantages and disadvantages of a rural way of life and where would you choose to live? We will publish the most interesting articles.*

Write your article.

1   Your readers live in the city. ☐
2   Write in a formal, academic style. ☐
3   Write about the negative aspects of living in the country. ☐
4   Write about the positive aspects of an urban lifestyle. ☐
5   Give the reader your opinion. ☐

B Read the model article and complete it with your own topic sentences.

The pluses and minuses of country living

(1) _____ Are you tired of the crowds, noise and pollution? Do you dream of open spaces, peace and quiet, and fresh air? You are not alone. Many city dwellers long to change their lives and move to the country. Some even manage it. But what are the realities of country living?

(2) _____ For a start, houses tend to be cheaper the further they are from the city. The air is cleaner and it is quieter. If you have children at school, you might find it friendlier than city schools. Your social life may also improve, as it is a well-known fact that in the country, unlike cities, you know everyone who lives nearby. Best of all, children can grow up running around outside, rather than cooped up in a flat in the city.

(3) _____ If you commute into the city, it might mean getting up much earlier and struggling with different forms of transport. Other disadvantages include having to drive children everywhere as public transport in the country tends to be inadequate. You might also find you miss the shops, restaurants and entertainment of the city.

(4) _____ Having spent many years in the city, I would love to get away from the concrete jungle and be surrounded by nature.

C Read and complete the writing task below.

You read the following announcement in an international magazine.

> *Tell us about your favourite place in your country. Where is it: inland, on the coast, in the mountains? Is it in the city, in a village or in the countryside? What is it like and what do people do when they go there? Would you recommend it to others?*

*Write your **article** in 220–260 words in an appropriate style.*

Watch the clock!

 Spend 5 minutes reading the task and planning your article.

 Spend 30 minutes writing your article.

 Spend 5 minutes checking and editing your article.

Remember!

There are many different reasons for writing an article. Your main aim could be to inform, to provide two sides to an argument, to compare and contrast or to describe a situation. The style you use will be dependent on the topic and aim of the article. See the Writing Reference for articles on page 184 of the Student's Book for further help.

Vocabulary

A Choose the correct answers.

1 The film was brilliant, quite ___ our expectations.
   a outshining
   b exceeding
   c overtaking
   d endeavouring

2 Apple was the Beatles' record ___.
   a brand
   b tape
   c licence
   d label

3 The party ___ in dancing to a live band.
   a terminated
   b concluded
   c culminated
   d climbed

4 I had to learn to ___ music when I took up the piano.
   a view
   b interpret
   c read
   d recite

5 I love his pastel ___ of fruit and flowers.
   a still lifes
   b portraits
   c portrayals
   b landscapes

6 The artist Salvador Dali was ___ in his day.
   a contrary
   b controversial
   c compliant
   d conceptual

7 Radiohead's ___ single, *Creep*, was released in 1992.
   a opening
   b primary
   c debut
   d introductory

8 I don't like ___ pop music. I prefer indie jazz and rock.
   a conservative
   b mundane
   c mainstream
   d average

9 I hate the way he blows his own ___ all the time.
   a horn
   b trumpet
   c flute
   d clarinet

10 Singing ___ harmony is harder than you think.
   a in
   b on
   c for
   d with

11 ___ biologists say whale numbers are decreasing.
   a Sea
   b Nautical
   c Marine
   d Oceanic

12 I would like to live in a ___ city like London.
   a cosmic
   b cosmopolitan
   c cosmographic
   d cosmetic

13 We are deeply ___ about the group's lack of funds.
   a concerning
   b conscious
   c cognitive
   d concerned

14 I'm glad to hear he has ___ in his final exams.
   a surpassed
   b outshone
   c headed
   d excelled

15 They ___ great hardship during the war.
   a struggled
   b juggled
   c endured
   d outdid

16 Study or you'll ___ your chances of passing.
   a ruin
   b break
   c demolish
   d raze

17 Luckily, everyone pulled ___ during the crisis.
   a apart
   b collectively
   c together
   d jointly

18 She never stops practising. She's ___ .
   a interacted
   b obsessed
   c obscured
   d irritable

19 I've failed too many times. I'm ___ the towel.
   a hitting on
   b burning up
   c keeping up
   d throwing in

20 I'm tired. I could ___ your nagging.
   a do without
   b wear down
   c get by
   d bounce back

Grammar

B Choose the correct answers.

1 This is smaller; it has ___ rooms as the other house.
   a half of
   b half as many
   c twice the
   d twice as many

2 The ___ you get there, the more likely you will get in.
   a earlier
   b earliest
   c more early
   d most early

3 The exams weren't ___ we'd expected.
   a hardly as hard as
   b almost so hard as
   c nearly as hard as
   d a bit hard as

4 It's ___ film I've ever seen.
   a the most extraordinary
   b more extraordinary than
   c most extraordinary
   d least extraordinary

5 They're ___ expensive, but much nicer.
   a pretty much
   b too much
   c enough
   d a little more

6 This job ___ for you. It's not stimulating.
   a is challenging enough
   b isn't challenging enough
   c is too challenging
   d isn't too challenging

7 ___ food to go around?
   a Was there too
   b Were there too
   c Wasn't there enough
   d Weren't there enough

8 He was delighted as he didn't usually get ___ .
   a so praise
   b such praise
   c so praising
   d such a praise

9 ___ was his joy, it was plain to see on his face.
   a So
   b Fairly
   c Most
   d Such

10 It was ___ a play that we left after the intermission.
   a such depressing
   b such depressed
   c so depressing
   d so depressed

11 Mark ___ a new job tomorrow.
   a is being interviewed for
   b was interviewing for
   c is going interview for
   d will be interviewed

12 I ___ a lift to the station so I didn't take the bus.
   a gave
   b am giving
   c was given
   d will be given

13 She hoped ___ a new job soon.
   a to offer
   b to be offered
   c be offered
   d being offered

14 It ___ that Tom was involved in the fraud.
   a alleged
   b is alleging
   c has alleged
   d has been alleged

15 We're ___ our decision to oppose the move.
   a asking reconsidering
   b being asked to reconsider
   c being reconsidered
   d asking to be reconsidered

16 Nobody ___ yet. We're the first.
   a seems to have arrived
   b seems to arrive
   c doesn't seem to arrive
   d is seeming to have arrived

17 They ___ the fact that he was incompetent.
   a didn't appear minding
   b appeared not minding
   c appeared not to mind
   d didn't appear mind

18 Poor Anita ___ in the airport.
   a had stolen her wallet
   b had her wallet stolen
   c was stealing her wallet
   d was being stolen her wallet

19 We ___ for years.
   a have had painted the house
   b haven't had painted the house
   c haven't had the house painted
   d haven't the house had painted

20 Sarah would like ___ before the party.
   a the windows cleaning
   b the windows to clean
   c have cleaned the windows
   d to have the windows cleaned

Review 5

Use of English

C Choose the correct answer.

SXSW

The South by Southwest music festival in Austin, Texas, is one of the largest festivals of its kind in the world, with the number of **(1)** ___ in recent years **(2)** ___ 2,000 performers. Commonly written as SXSW, the festival **(3)** ___ in 1987 and took its name from the famous Hitchcock film *North by Northwest* as a play on words. The festival's **(4)** ___ was created from the desire of local organisers to feature bands who play outside of **(5)** ___ music, who instead play alternative music, a genre that matches the musical **(6)** ___ of many Austinites. The festival began with a somewhat **(7)** ___, easy-going feel that is characteristic of Austin, but as the festival has drawn more attention over the years, the pace has become quite busy and **(8)** ___, to the delight of organisers. Also pleased are the performers, as some musicians who played in SXSW soon found themselves under **(9)** ___ with major record **(10)** ___ after giving talented, **(11)** ___ performances. The festival's success has been a major boon for the city of Austin, as the event attracts important industry people as well as spectators, all of whom descend on the city for ten days, doing much to **(12)** ___ the local economy.

1	**a**	commissions	**b**	exhibitions	**c**	subjects	**d**	participants
2	**a**	exceeding	**b**	erasing	**c**	catering	**d**	demanding
3	**a**	covered	**b**	debuted	**c**	copied	**d**	listed
4	**a**	concept	**b**	controversy	**c**	movement	**d**	landscape
5	**a**	background	**b**	lead	**c**	front	**d**	mainstream
6	**a**	feelings	**b**	tastes	**c**	sights	**d**	sounds
7	**a**	reasonable	**b**	unsophisticated	**c**	sedentary	**d**	relaxed
8	**a**	pricey	**b**	hectic	**c**	provincial	**d**	solitary
9	**a**	approval	**b**	harmony	**c**	contract	**d**	display
10	**a**	labels	**b**	lyrics	**c**	verses	**d**	beats
11	**a**	energetic	**b**	highbrow	**c**	fragile	**d**	formative
12	**a**	mushroom	**b**	stimulate	**c**	boast	**d**	endeavour

D Complete the text by writing one word in each gap.

Napping

We know sleep is an activity we can't do **(1)** _____, yet we let our hectic lifestyles wear us **(2)** _____ until we can't rise from bed in the morning. We know **(3)** _____ longer we go without sleep, the more likely we are to have an accident, and when that happens, we've hit rock **(4)** _____. It's safe to **(5)** _____ that too many people have come up **(6)** _____ this problem. But there's no need for us to run ourselves into the **(7)** _____ over a lack of sleep. Now it seems as **(8)** _____ people are bouncing **(9)** _____ from this sleepless torture by taking mid-day naps. Some may think it makes them look lazy to the boss, but employers these days aren't as old-fashioned **(10)** _____ we might expect, and **(11)** _____ ideas as napping at work are catching on. It's been proven **(12)** _____ researchers that a mid-day nap increases productivity, and more employers are **(13)** _____ their tune about the practice. So if you're lacking sleep, don't **(14)** _____ in the towel just yet. Keep your head **(15)** _____ water and hopefully the mid-day nap will be the routine at your workplace soon.

E Think of one word only that can be used appropriately in all three sentences.

1 There's a new theatre _____ this weekend – we should go!

I wasn't so pleased with the _____ act at the concert.

If you want to work at my company, there's a(n) _____ in the sales department.

2 If you look at this _____, you can see that the company's numbers are down.

Captain, you must _____ a new course soon – there's a storm coming from that direction.

Her single made it to the very top of the dance _____ in the UK last summer.

3 Those kids behave very badly because they are _____ by their parents.

Don't drink that milk – it's _____ and it will make you sick.

Lisa _____ our fun with her constant complaining about work.

4 Some farmers leave their work in the _____ for a job in the city.

The soldier was awarded a medal for his bravery on the _____ of battle.

I'm not familiar with this concept, as it's not in my _____ of study.

5 This is your third singing job this week? What a _____ of luck!

The painter used a long brush _____ to create clouds on the canvas.

If you _____ the back of a cat gently, it will likely make purring noises.

F Complete the second sentences so that they have a similar meaning to the first sentences using the words in bold. Use between three and six words.

1 What I'd really like to hear is the sound of the last school bell.

EARS

To hear the sound of the last school bell _____.

2 This studio is lacking in places to sit and paint.

ENOUGH

There _____ and paint in the studio.

3 The stage curtains are in need of repairing.

BE

We _____ repaired.

4 People didn't attend the concert because it was so long.

AS

The concert was so _____ off from attending.

5 The tickets will cost more if you sit at the front.

EXPENSIVE

The closer we sit to the front, _____ be.

6 She asked the staff to put her paintings up at the gallery.

HAVING

She is _____ display at the gallery.

7 The event was cancelled due to lack of participants.

FEW

There _____ the event was cancelled.

8 People started arguing over the project because it was very confusing.

SO

It _____ people started arguing over it.

Reading

You are going to read three extracts which are all concerned some way with sport. For questions 1–6, choose the best answer (a, b, c or d) which fits best according to the text.

Sussex Summer Tennis Academy

The programme

With 35 hours of tennis per week, Sussex Summer Tennis Academy (SSTA) offers one of the most intensive tennis programmes in the world. Our staff, who are all former professional players and coaches, provide comprehensive, high-level coaching. The low ratio of players to coaches (4 to 1) ensures that all players benefit from our professional training methods.

Our training programme integrates tennis drills, match-play situations and physical conditioning (speed, strength and coordination) to provide an all-round experience that will take you to the next level.

After the daily training sessions, players can relax in our spa or swimming pool or participate in various leisure activities inside and outside the academy.

The location

Located near Brighton and Hove, Sussex, in the south of England, SSTA enjoys a wonderful location and climate. But on those few days when the weather lets us down, we have a large number of indoor courts that allows the training to continue uninterrupted.

The Sussex coast also benefits from a beautiful natural landscape, including many miles of sand or pebble beaches, as well as from the proximity of the thriving cosmopolitan city of Brighton and Hove.

The Academy

SSTA facilities include:

- 20 tennis courts (12 outdoor and 8 indoor)
- Fitness room
- Swimming pool
- Spa

A Walk on the Wild Side

There are a few issues that you should think about when shopping at Hikeright.

Cost

With some outdoor gear, you might not need the fanciest or most expensive piece of kit out there. However, we're talking about your feet here, and saving money is not as important as keeping your feet comfortable. So, our advice is not to look at the price when you're trying on our boots.

Comfort

Find the pair of boots that fit your feet best and that do the job you want them to do. Listen to your feet. They will tell you if they are not 100% comfortable. Here at Hikeright, we are so concerned about your feet that we allow you to take our boots away for up to a month to try them out at home. If you're not happy, simply bring them back within one month (in clean, saleable condition!) for an exchange or a full refund.

The right footwear for the job

There is no such thing as the perfect hiking boot. For light walking in the summer over easy terrain, you'll only need a pair of sandals or trail shoes. However, if you're going to be going off-trail on long hikes over rough terrain, then you'll need a pair of heavy off-trail boots. Our specially trained staff will be happy to advise you on the right footwear for the job.

Motivating Children to do Sports

Encouraging children to participate in sports helps them develop a healthy lifestyle. However, it's easy to cross the line between encouraging children and pushing them beyond their own abilities, so here are some simple rules to help you get the balance right.

- The biggest motivation for kids is having fun, so encourage your child to take part in any sport that he or she enjoys.
- Focus on participation rather than on winning. If you expect your child to win every time, you will only create anxiety and lessen their enjoyment.
- Allow your child to make mistakes. Making mistakes is part of learning, and if you are too critical you will put your child off.
- You don't have to do the sport that your child chooses, but do try to enjoy what your child does. If you show interest and give support, your child will grow in confidence and will be more likely to improve.
- Children often need help setting goals. Therefore, encourage your child to set realistic and attainable goals and to measure his or her progress.
- When your child loses at a competitive sport, don't blame the referee, the weather or the equipment. However, do try to focus on the positives in your child's performance.

1 The purpose of the first text is to
   a persuade people to take up tennis.
   b promote a place where tennis is taught.
   c convince people to go to Sussex on holiday.
   d encourage people to use certain facilities.

2 What is provided on the tennis course?
   a an opportunity to play against professionals
   b an option to play tennis, swim or relax in the spa
   c the chance to greatly improve your playing ability
   d a holiday at the seaside including tennis coaching

3 You should buy your boots at Hikeright because
   a they have good boots at cheap prices.
   b boots worn outdoors can be returned.
   c they encourage hiking in them for a month.
   d they make sure you end up with the best boots.

4 When buying boots, your main aim should be
   a to find the most comfortable pair.
   b to find the right boots at the right price.
   c to consider when you'll be wearing the boots.
   d to find the perfect all round boots.

5 The third text is aimed
   a primarily at parents and carers.
   b at children taking up a sport.
   c at sports teachers.
   d at coaches and referees.

6 When motivating children, you should focus on
   a pointing out other people's mistakes.
   b setting goals and achieving them.
   c enjoyment, participation and positive feedback.
   d winning and increasing confidence.

Vocabulary

A Complete the sentences with the correct form of the words.

1 His fear of being injured again was a real _____ to getting back into the game.   **HINDER**

2 His excellent _____ of the Tour de France doping scandal earned him a prestigious award in sports journalism.   **COVER**

3 Nadia Comaneci's _____ performances at the 1976 Olympics earned her the first ever perfect score of 10 in women's gymnastics.   **DAZZLE**

4 _____ interviews was the most satisfying part of his job.   **CONDUCT**

5 Michael Phelps is the world-record _____ for the 100 and 200-metre butterfly and the 400-metre individual medley.   **HOLD**

6 Few players have shown more _____ to the game of tennis than Roger Federer and Novak Djokovic.   **DEDICATE**

B Circle the correct words.

Cheats never prosper

I was lucky enough to get a ticket for an under-21 International Athletics Competition, held recently at the National Sports Centre. It was a very exciting day and there was a great atmosphere. The crowd **(1)** cheered / encouraged during each event and, even when one of the athletes was injured and had to be helped from the track, there was respectful **(2)** applause / praise.

However, there was one unfortunate incident that rather spoiled things for me. It occurred during the 4 x 400 metre **(3)** passing / relay race. At the start of the final **(4)** circle / lap as a runner was trying to pass the **(5)** baton / club to his team mate, one of the runners on a different team deliberately **(6)** interfered / obstructed the handover, effectively putting that team out of the race.

At first, I wasn't sure that any of the officials had seen what happened, but after a short delay I read on the scoreboard that the team who had cheated had been **(7)** disabled / disqualified. The incident was reported in one of the national newspapers where I read that the athlete who had cheated could face a lifetime **(8)** ban / refusal from athletics competitions.

C Complete the sentences with these prepositions

> back   for   off   on   up (x2)   out (x2)

1 Although she got _____ to a good start, she lost the race as she couldn't keep up the pace.
2 Beatrice couldn't believe that everything she'd worked so hard _____ was now gone.
3 They're too far ahead now. You won't be able to catch _____ unless you run very fast.
4 She was in second place for most of the race, but then dropped _____ to fourth and finished there.
5 Unfortunately, Nadal had a serious injury and was forced to pull _____ of various competitions.
6 The reason you're stiff now is that you didn't warm _____ before going on such a long run.
7 After he was knocked _____ in the first round, Eric never boxed again.
8 Even though Harriet knew her team would lose, she inspired them to fight _____ until the bitter end.

D Choose the correct answers.

1 As long as I've got Mrs Jenkins ___, I know I can succeed.
   a in my corner   **b** in my house   **c** in my spot

2 She's ___ thanks to the amount of exercise she does every day.
   a improved   **b** in great shape   **c** in good figure

3 Alex got off to ___ this year at school. Let's hope he keeps it up.
   a a great beginning   **b** an advantage   **c** a good start

4 Annie's efforts to cut her spending fell ___ when her car broke down and she had to have it fixed.
   a at the first hurdle   **b** at the first gate   **c** on the first bend

5 Nadia's training came to ___ when she broke her arm.
   a a sudden arrest   **b** a sudden halt   **c** a short halt

6 Tracy hit ___ when she said the problem was a lack of fitness.
   a the nail head   **b** the bull's-eye   **c** the sheep's-eye

7 We've made them an offer for the furniture. Now the ball's ___. We'll just have to wait and see if they decide to accept.
   a on their side   **b** in their court   **c** on their turf

8 Despite being first ___ with their new high-performance sportswear, they were unable to make a profit from it.
   a in line   **b** out of the house   **c** out of the gate

Grammar

A Match the quotes (1–6) and the reported sentences (a–f).

1 'I'm so sorry I missed the shot.' ☐
2 'I didn't miss the shot!' ☐
3 'Well done for not missing the shot.' ☐
4 'OK, you're right! I did miss the shot.' ☐
5 'No! No! No! I didn't miss the shot!' ☐
6 'It wasn't me who missed the shot. It was him.' ☐

a She congratulated him on not missing the shot.
b He insisted that he hadn't missed the shot.
c He apologised for missing the shot.
d He accused him of missing the shot.
e He admitted missing the shot.
f He denied missing the shot.

B Complete the quotes.

1 'Don't _____.'
   Our teacher told us not to forget to bring our trainers the following day.

2 'You _____ fit enough.'
   The coach said we'd train for an hour every day until we were fit enough.

3 'Can _____?'
   She asked the coach if she could join the basketball team the following term.

4 'Shall _____?'
   They asked their trainer if they should put away the equipment then.

5 'I _____.'
   She told her fellow swimmers she'd meet them at the pool at eight that night.

6 'Please _____ health certificates.'
   Mr Smith asked them to bring him their health certificates.

C Complete the sentences with these reporting verbs in the correct form.

advise   apologise   complain   decide   encourage   offer   warn   promise

1 Anne: Don't worry, I'll help you put up the nets before the others arrive.
   Anne _____ the nets before the others arrived.

2 Bill: I think you should warm up before you start playing.
   Bill _____ playing.

3 Lisa: OK, I won't get the green sweatshirt, I'll buy the red one.
   Lisa _____ but to buy the red one.

4 Fred: I'll be here at 10.30 on the dot. You have my word.
   Fred _____ on the dot.

5 Paula: Stella always arrives too late to help set up the equipment. It's really annoying.
   Paula _____ to help set up the equipment.

6 Tony: I'm so sorry I missed the training session.
   Tony _____ the training session.

7 Wendy: Seriously, you're a fantastic swimmer. You really must join a swimming club.
   Wendy _____ a swimming club.

8 Sam: Don't overdo the stretches in your first yoga class as you could easily injure yourself.
   Sam _____ in my first yoga class as I could easily injure myself.

D Complete the reported questions.

1 'Have you brought your swimming costume?' asked Ruby.
   Ruby asked me _____ swimming costume.

2 'Why aren't you playing football with the other boys?' Jim asked Charlie.
   Jim asked Charlie _____ with the other boys.

3 'When are you going on the rugby tour to France?' Philip asked Rob.
   Philip wanted to know _____ the rugby tour to France.

4 'How are you getting to the training session tomorrow?' Emily asked Sarah.
   Emily asked _____ to the training session the following day.

5 'Did your team win?' Frank asked his son.
   Frank wanted to know _____.

6 'Do you know where the team is staying during the European Games?' Laura asked Vincent.
   Laura asked _____ during the European Games.

7 'Where's my tennis racket?' Mark asked his mother.
   Mark asked _____.

8 'Why don't you like cycling?' Rose asked Tina.
   Rose wanted _____ cycling.

Listening

You will hear three different extracts. For questions 1–6, choose the best answer, a, b or c. There are two questions for each extract.

Extract One

You hear two people talking about underwater hockey.

1 What does Hannah think of underwater hockey?
  a It's just like hockey.
  b Her team is unbeatable.
  c It's tougher than hockey.

2 What does Hannah do to improve her game?
  a She wears fins, a diving mask and snorkel.
  b She practises holding her breath.
  c She swims every day.

Extract Two

You hear part of an interview with a young tennis player.

3 His father wasn't a professional player because
  a he didn't have the talent.
  b he had to get a job instead.
  c he didn't take advantage of his opportunities.

4 What is Steve doing now to improve his chances?
  a He's being coached by his father and he's got a fitness trainer.
  b He's lifting lots of weights and working on his backhand.
  c He allows his father to push him to the limit.

Extract Three

You hear part of an interview with a former Olympic rower.

5 What was Robin's routine before he retired?
  a He'd train every weekday and have the weekend off.
  b He'd spend most of his time in the gym.
  c He'd get up early, train for several hours and take a day off a week.

6 In Robin's opinion, what is his greatest achievement?
  a his Olympic gold medals
  b his environmental campaign
  c his long career as an athlete

Writing

A Read the writing task below and answer the questions.

> You work in an international college in the UK. Your college principal, Mrs Jones, has received a letter from a teenage student, Simon Perez, who is coming to the college for a term and wants to know about sports facilities, as he is training for an expedition in the Andes. You've been asked to reply.
>
> Read the extract from the letter and the comments from the principal. Then, using the information appropriately, write a letter to Simon explaining what facilities are available.

> As well as improving my language skills, I need to make sure I increase my fitness so that I'll be ready for an expedition to the Andes in February. What facilities are available in the college and in the nearby town?
>
> • In college: climbing wall, gym, running track, football pitches and basketball courts
> • In town: Olympic size swimming pool, tennis courts, skate park

Write your letter. You should use your own words as far as possible.

1 Who will be reading your letter?
2 What will you say in the first paragraph?
3 Apart from the introduction and conclusion, how many paragraphs should it have?
4 How formal should your letter be?

B Read the model letter and complete it with these words.

additionally   available   charge   delighted   forward   instructor   regarding   satisfactory

Dear Simon

Mrs Jones has asked me to write to you **(1)** _____ your request for information on sports facilities in the college and in our town.

I am **(2)** _____ to inform you that there are very good sports facilities in college, which I hope will meet your needs. We have a brand new climbing wall, which is proving very popular with our students. There are sessions with a(n) **(3)** _____ every morning and free sessions in the afternoon and early evening. We also have a running track, football pitches and basketball courts. There are clubs for all of these sports. **(4)** _____, there is a state-of-the-art gym, which is open 24 hours a day.

Other facilities, not **(5)** _____ in college, can be found in town, which is a 15-minute bus ride away. There is a leisure centre with an Olympic size swimming pool and three tennis courts. And there is a very popular skate park at the other end of town, with more tennis courts nearby. All are free of **(6)** _____ for students.

I hope this answers your question and you find our sports facilities **(7)** _____. We look **(8)** _____ to welcoming you to the college in September.

Best wishes

Susan Field

C Read and complete the writing task below.

You've received a letter from your friend Teresa who is coming to stay in your town and wants to know about sports facilities, as she is training to get into her university basketball team.

Read the extract from the letter and the notes added below. Then, using the information appropriately, write a letter to Teresa explaining what facilities are available.

I need to make sure I keep up my fitness so that I have a chance of getting into the basketball team when I go home. As you know, it's my dream! Can you give me an idea of the sports facilities in your town? I'm really looking forward to seeing you and spending some time hanging out together.

- leisure centre with swimming pool, squash courts and gym
- aerobics and yoga classes
- basketball courts 20 minutes away by bus
- running track 10-minute walk away

*Write your **letter** in 180–220 words in an appropriate style.*

Remember!

When writing a letter, remember to state the reason you're writing and make sure you respond to all the questions or requests made in the input material. Use the appropriate register for the person you are writing to and don't forget to use the correct conventions for opening and closing a letter. See the Writing Reference for letters on page 185 of the Student's Book for further help.

Watch the clock!

 Spend 5 minutes reading the task and planning your letter.

 Spend 30 minutes writing your letter.

 Spend 5 minutes checking and editing your letter.

Reading

Five paragraphs have been removed from the text. Choose from the paragraphs A–F the one which fits each gap (1–5). There is one extra paragraph which you do not need to use.

Nano's big future

'I sit before you today with very little hair on my head. It fell out a few weeks ago as a result of the chemotherapy I've been undergoing. Twenty years ago, without even this crude chemotherapy, I would already be dead. But 20 years from now, nanoscale missiles will target cancer cells in the human body and leave everything else blissfully alone. I may not live to see it. But I am confident it will happen.' Richard Smalley spoke these words on June 22, 1999. He died of non-Hodgkin's lymphoma on October 28, 2005. The 62-year-old Nobel Prize-winning chemist was a nanotech pioneer, one of the first to see the approaching 'technological tsunami'. **1**

Nanotechnology has been around for two decades, but the first wave of applications is only now beginning to break. As it does, it will make the computer revolution look like small change. It will affect everything from the batteries we use to the clothes we wear to the way we treat cancer. But what makes it so special? **2**

Joking aside, nanotechnology matters because familiar materials begin to develop odd properties when they're nanosize. Tear a piece of aluminium foil into tiny strips, and it will still behave like aluminium — even after the strips have become so small that you need a microscope to see them. But keep chopping them smaller, and at some point — 20 to 30 nanometers, in this case — the pieces can explode. **3**

Substances behave magically at the nanoscale because that's where the essential properties of matter are determined. Arrange calcium carbonate molecules in a sawtooth pattern, for instance, and you get fragile, crumbly chalk. Stack the same molecules like bricks, and they help form the layers of the tough, iridescent shell of an abalone. **4**

'Nano's going to be like the invention of plastic,' says Paul Alivisatos, associate director of physical sciences at Lawrence Berkeley National Laboratory's new nanofabrication centre. 'It'll be everywhere: in the scalpels doctors use for surgery and in the fabrics we wear.' Alivisatos already owns a pair of stain-resistant nanopants from the Gap, made from fibres treated with fluorinated nanopolymer. 'I spilled coffee on them this morning, and it rolled right off.' **5**

Nanotechnology may not have saved Richard Smalley, but it will save others. It is evolving incredibly quickly. Many of the current applications would have seemed pretty unrealistic even ten years ago.

A It's a tantalizing idea: creating a material with ideal properties by customising its atomic structure. Scientists have already developed rarefied tools, such as the scanning tunnelling microscope, capable of viewing and moving individual atoms via an exquisitely honed tip just one atom wide.

B One reason for the rapid global spread of nanotechnology is that the entry cost is comparatively low. Countries that missed out on the computer revolution because they lacked the capital to build vast, high-tech factories that make silicon chips are less likely to miss the nanotech wave.

C A tsunami is unnoticeable in the open ocean – a long, low wave whose power becomes clear only when it reaches shore and breaks. Technological revolutions travel with the same stealth. Spotting the wave while it's still crossing the ocean is tricky, which explains why so few of us are aware of the one that's approaching.

D Not all nanosize materials change properties so usefully (there's talk of adding nano aluminium to rocket fuel), but the fact that some do is a boon. With them, scientists can engineer a cornucopia of exotic new materials, such as plastic that conducts electricity and coatings that prevent iron from rusting. It's like you shrink a cat and keep shrinking it, and then at some point, all at once, as if by magic, it turns into a dog.

E Such commercial applications continue to spread. Homeowners now have the option of installing windows manufactured by PPG Industries, a company that uses nanoscale particles of titanium dioxide to make glass that doesn't streak and never needs washing. Food companies have begun experimenting with nanopackaging that changes color when food spoils or contains bacteria.

F The main thing to know about nanotechnology is that it's small. Really small. Nano, a prefix that means 'dwarf' in Greek, is shorthand for nanometer, one-billionth of a metre: a distance so minute that comparing it to anything in the regular world is a bit of a joke.

Vocabulary

A Complete the words in the sentences.

1 Oscar has an entrepreneurial streak. He's made a k _ _ _ _ _ _ selling his latest invention on the Internet.
2 Although we don't know what the future h _ _ _ _, it's quite likely that many different cancers will become curable.
3 Her time in Chile helped s _ _ _ _ her future. She wouldn't have got this job if she couldn't speak Spanish.
4 We thought we'd be able to p _ _ _ _ _ _ the outcome of the experiment, but we were on the wrong track.
5 I had a h _ _ _ _ that Lorna would win the election, but not by such a massive majority.
6 The tenants had to pay out of their own p _ _ _ _ _ _ to repair the damage to the flat.

B Complete the sentences with these words.

eternity   guess   infinite   omen   posterity   speculate

1 We can only _____ about the reasons why the two planes collided. We'll have to wait for the results of the air crash investigation.
2 Until we have all the facts, we can only make an educated _____ as to why the engine failed.
3 As a child, the summer holidays felt like a(n) _____. Now they go by like a flash.
4 In many societies, seeing a comet in the night sky used to be considered a bad _____. In others, it was thought to bring good luck.
5 At the age of seventy, he planted an arboretum for _____, knowing full well he would never see his trees reach maturity.
6 Albert Einstein is believed to have said, 'Only two things are _____, the universe and human stupidity, and I'm not sure about the former.'

C Circle the correct words.

UN Warning

With the population of the world **(1)** likely / inevitably to grow to nearly nine billion by 2040, experts are warning that we are rapidly running out of time to ensure that there will be enough resources to meet our **(2)** anticipated / perpetual needs.

According to the UN, the world is going need at least 50% more food, 45% more energy and 30% more water by 2030.

'Despite the **(3)** looming / promising catastrophe, little action is being taken to set sustainable development goals,' said a UN spokesman. 'The situation is already **(4)** critical / unforeseen. There is no time to waste.'

The UN's warning is **(5)** intended / fated to mobilise governments to take immediate action to **(6)** preserve / reserve resources and manage energy consumption more efficiently.

D Match the phrases 1–6 to the phrases a–f.

1 Medical advances have given rise ☐
2 There has yet to be a breakthrough ☐
3 Cases of influenza have increased ☐
4 Carla has always been ☐
5 There hasn't been any improvement ☐
6 Before going into science, he was about ☐

a in the search for a cure for dementia.
b in her health since she saw the doctor.
c to the likelihood of people living to 100.
d of the opinion that exercise is vital.
e to accept a job in banking.
f by 25% this winter.

12 Fast Forward

Grammar

A Complete the text with these phrases.

a to overcome this problem
b to make it possible for robots
c while most of us think of
d to do that

e since cockroaches have
f to see how cockroaches use their antennae
g however
h in order to enable the machine

Cockroaches inspire robot antenna

(1) ___ cockroaches as a nasty nuisance, to a team of engineers at Johns Hopkins University in Baltimore, Maryland, the pesky beasties are excellent role models. (2) ___ such sophisticated and sensitive antennae, scientists decided to use them as a model when building an antenna for a robot. The sensor-laden antenna they built resembles a cockroach's navigational appendage. The antenna sends signals to the robot's electronic brain (3) ___ to scurry along walls, turn corners, and avoid obstacles, just like a cockroach. The technology could provide an important navigational alternative (4) ___ to be dispatched into dangerous locations, such as collapsed buildings. At present, most robotic vehicles rely on artificial vision or sonar systems for their navigation. (5) ___ , robotic eyes don't operate well in low light, and sonar systems can be confused by polished surfaces. (6) ___ , assistant professor Noah Cowan and his colleagues have built a crude antenna prototype based on the navigational techniques of a cockroach. When a robot navigates with a sense of touch 'there is nothing that has to travel through the air that can be interfered with by substances like dust or smoke,' said Cowan. His team studied cockroach locomotion (7) ___ to track along walls in the dark. (8) ___ , the engineers built an oval-shaped 'obstacle course' for the cockroaches, and then filmed the insects as they manoeuvered inside it. 'Every time I looked at the images of the runs, I was in awe of the cockroaches' agility and speed,' said Jusuk Lee, a Ph.D. student who collected the data.

B Choose the correct answers.

1 ___ a technical fault, we are unable to connect you to the Internet.
 a Owing in   b Owing to   c Owing with

2 ___ you haven't been able to get to the supermarket today, I think we should go out to dinner.
 a Seeing that   b Seen that   c Since that

3 ___ an increase in greenhouse gases, the world is getting hotter.
 a Due with   b Due in   c Due to

4 There wasn't ___ data to determine whether the experiment had been successful.
 a too   b enough   c so

5 ___ not earning much money, they managed to enjoy quite a high standard of living.
 a In spite   b Even though   c Despite

6 Microscopes are used ___ at things you can't see with the naked eye.
 a for looking   b to looking   c so look

7 The formula was ___ that she couldn't remember it the next day.
 a too complicated   b so complicated   c complicated enough

8 ___ Lucas was hoping to study chemistry at university, his brother had decided to apply for a job straight from school.
 a However   b While   c In spite of

C Complete the second sentences so that they have a similar meaning to the first sentences.

1 Betty wanted to go to law school, so she worked very hard for her exams.

Betty _____ for her exams _____.

2 With all the competition these days, it's very difficult for young people to get a job.

Since there _____ these days, young people
_____ to get a job.

3 No classrooms will be renovated in the foreseeable future because of budget cuts.

Due _____, they _____ any classrooms in the foreseeable future.

4 We're not surprised that Camilla is feeling stressed as she has so many decisions to make very quickly.

With _____, it's not _____ stressed.

5 It is unlikely that we will be able to afford to buy a house soon due to price rises in the construction industry.

Owing _____ in the construction industry, we are
_____ to afford to buy a house soon.

6 You handed in your work late, so you can't expect to get it back any time soon.

Seeing _____ your work late, _____ to get it back any time soon

D Circle the correct words.

1 Either / Neither we stay in and watch a film or we go to the cinema.
2 I don't think neither / either of those solutions will work.
3 Neither / Nor of them wants to admit it was their fault.
4 Neither Claudia or / nor Lucy is going to drive tonight.
5 I doubt either / neither subject will be easy, but I think I'm better at Maths.
6 Either of / Neither of his sons followed in his footsteps.

E Match the phrases 1–8 to the phrases a–h.

1 Either you borrow my book or ☐	a	neither did her sister.
2 Neither Louisa nor Joseph ☐	b	or I will.
3 They will neither drive nor cycle to the park; ☐	c	they'll have to walk.
4 We'll either drive you to the park now or ☐	d	you buy your own. It's up to you.
5 Either one of us could get the job; ☐	e	are going to the party.
6 Serena didn't want to cook a meal; ☐	f	we'll have to wait and see.
7 Neither Rosie nor her friends ☐	g	is prepared to buy the books.
8 Either Dominic will collect you from school ☐	h	you'll have to walk there later.

Listening

You will hear someone talking about geothermal energy. For questions 1–8, complete the sentences.

1 Geothermal energy originates beneath the _____ of the earth.

2 Mankind has benefited from bathing in _____ for thousands of years.

3 Geothermal energy can be used to _____ dwellings and work places, as well as to generate electricity.

4 Geothermal heat pumps can help cool a building in summer because they can _____ heat back to the ground.

5 In winter, hot water from under the ground can be used to warm up roads and pavements in order to _____ snow.

6 Geothermal electricity is generated by digging deep _____ and tapping steam and hot water that drive turbines.

7 The country that produces the greatest amount of geothermal energy is _____.

8 Iceland is planning to _____ its renewable energy to other countries in order to advance its economic recovery.

Writing

A Read the writing task below and write T (true) or F (false).

Following a class discussion, your teacher has asked you to write an essay giving your views on this topic.

> *'Although sustainable agriculture in the 21st century could lead to better farming practices, will it ensure that enough food is produced for a growing population?' Discuss.*

Write your essay.

1 Your essay should describe only the advantages of sustainable farming. ☐

2 You should write about what sustainable farming means. ☐

3 Your essay should be about the advantages and disadvantages of sustainable farming. ☐

4 You shouldn't mention industrial farming. ☐

5 End your essay by giving your opinion on sustainable agriculture in the 21st century. ☐

B Read the model essay and complete it with these phrases and sentences.

   a Critics of sustainable agriculture claim that its methods will result in fewer crops and increased land use.

   b Sustainable agriculture takes many forms

   c On the other hand, if sustainable agriculture is introduced extensively in the 21st century, it will involve a wide range of techniques

   d The industrial approach relies on the cultivation of a single crop

Sustainable agriculture in the 21st century

(1) ___, but the main idea behind it is a rejection of the industrial approach to food production developed during the 20th century.

(2) ___, mechanisation, chemical pesticides and fertilisers, and biotechnology. Although it may sound environmentally unfriendly, we cannot ignore the fact that this approach has made food plentiful and affordable. However, the ecological and social price has been high: soil erosion and contamination, water contamination, loss of biodiversity, deforestation and the decline of the family farm.

(3) ___, including organic and free-range. These methods are like natural ecological processes. Farmers will have healthy soil by planting fields with different crops year after year, and they will avoid using pesticides by encouraging the presence of organisms that control pests which destroy crops.

(4) ___They add that a commitment to its practices will mean inevitable food shortages for a world population expected to exceed eight billion by the year 2030. There's recent evidence, though, suggesting that over time, sustainably farmed lands can be as productive as conventional industrial farms. We will have to wait and see.

C Read and complete the writing task below.

Following a class discussion, your teacher has asked you to write an essay giving your views on this topic.

> 'As the world's population grows and economic and environmental difficulties multiply, only technology will be able to provide solutions to our global problems.' Discuss.

*Write your **essay** in 220–260 words in an appropriate style.*

Watch the clock!

 Spend 5 minutes reading the task and planning your essay.

 Spend 30 minutes writing your essay.

 Spend 5 minutes checking and editing your essay.

Remember!

When you are writing an essay, spend some time thinking about the topic and writing notes before you start. Make sure you show both sides of an argument and provide examples to support your claims. Use your concluding paragraph to give your opinion. See the Writing Reference for essays on page 186 of the Student's Book for further help.

Vocabulary

A Choose the correct answers.

1 Jason is a radio and television sports ___.
   a commander
   b commentator
   c conductor
   d leader

2 Good luck, Selma. We're all ___ for you.
   a rooting
   b reviving
   c dashing
   d pitching

3 The cast delivered a ___ performance last night.
   a capturing
   b cultivating
   c competing
   d captivating

4 I've swum twenty ___ of the pool today.
   a lanes
   b lines
   c laps
   d rows

5 They played better than us and we were ___.
   a conquered
   b bounced
   c thrashed
   d pitched

6 You pulled a muscle because you didn't ___ properly.
   a warm up
   b warm in
   c heat up
   d work out

7 I didn't ___ a good start and I couldn't catch up.
   a go off to
   b get off to
   c lead off to
   d set off to

8 Nobody helped her. She did it ___.
   a for herself
   b by her own
   c with her own
   d on her own

9 I can't do anymore. The ball's in his ___ now.
   a square
   b pitch
   c court
   d course

10 He works out so he's ___ great shape.
   a at
   b in
   c on
   d for

11 Nobody knows what the future ___.
   a holds
   b enjoys
   c delivers
   d gains

12 I can only ___ about his reasons for resigning.
   a contemplate
   b reflect
   c conjecture
   d speculate

13 The show was cancelled due to an ___ event.
   a unpredictable
   b unforeseen
   c innovative
   d anticipated

14 There are ___ storm clouds in the sky.
   a perpetual
   b unaware
   c menacing
   d timeless

15 After I pay my bills, I have little ___ income.
   a reusable
   b unavoidable
   c disposable
   d preceding

16 The good news is that his salary has ___ 20%.
   a increased by
   b increased for
   c given rise to
   d improved in

17 Has genetic ___ increased crop yields?
   a production
   b manufacturing
   c development
   d engineering

18 The ___ telecommunications market is growing.
   a wired
   b wireless
   c portable
   d fixed

19 We want a return to the ___ economy of the past.
   a booming
   b failing
   c listless
   d energetic

20 A cure for cancer would be a scientific ___.
   a expansion
   b extension
   c breakthrough
   d growth

Grammar

B Choose the correct answers.

1 I ___ Harry I'd be late.
   a say
   b said
   c tell
   d told

2 Paul said that he wouldn't ___ help.
   a able to
   b be able
   c be able to
   d been able to

3 We explained we'd be leaving the ___.
   a tomorrow
   b yesterday
   c following day
   d day following

4 Mary told me she ___ revise at the weekend.
   a must
   b mustn't
   c hadn't
   d had to

5 She promised they definitely ___ on holiday.
   a had gone
   b would go
   c went
   d didn't go

6 Robert admitted ___ in the exam.
   a to cheat
   b cheating
   c have cheated
   d not cheat

7 Rebecca insisted ___ for our meal.
   a on paying
   b of paying
   c to pay
   d for paying

8 Carl is refusing ___ the contract.
   a on signing
   b of signing
   c to sign
   d for signing

9 We congratulated Jonathan ___ second in the race.
   a on coming
   b of coming
   c to come
   d for coming

10 They apologised ___ so late.
   a that arrived
   b of arriving
   c to arrive
   d for arriving

11 ___ a bank error, I was credited £1000!
   a Owing to
   b Seeing that
   c Since
   d With

12 We should stay now ___ we're already here.
   a owing to
   b seeing as
   c because of
   d due to

13 These instructions aren't ___ for the children to follow.
   a such clear
   b enough clear
   c clear enough
   d so little clear

14 ___ achieve his goal, he had to focus on training.
   a So that
   b In order
   c In order for
   d In order to

15 Melissa refused to stay in bed ___ feeling exhausted.
   a however
   b whereas
   c despite
   d nevertheless

16 We enjoyed our walk ___ the rain.
   a in spite of
   b whereas
   c though
   d while

17 They neither praised ___ his work.
   a or criticised
   b nor criticised
   c neither criticised
   d not criticised

18 Daniel wasn't qualified for he job. ___, he was chosen.
   a Even though
   b Whereas
   c Nevertheless
   d In spite of

19 Neither Ruth nor Carrie ___ for a second interview.
   a has invited
   b have invited
   c has been invited
   d have been invited

20 Simon doesn't want to move and ___.
   a we don't either
   b we don't neither
   c we neither do
   d we aren't either

Use of English

C Complete the text with the correct form of the words.

Sports mad

Many sports **(1)** _____ – and not the average follower, but the ones   FAN

who go to great lengths to show their love for the sport – make us scratch our

heads and wonder why some people have such a **(2)** _____ desire to   BURN

watch sport. One of the answers lies in the make-up of our brain and how

we as **(3)** _____ respond when we view competitions. The human brain   OBSERVE

has chemicals that are triggered when a feeling of excitement or anger occurs;

these chemicals **(4)** _____ our bodies and sometimes make us behave   POWER

like **(5)** _____. When our team scores a goal or, conversely, when   MANIC

one of our players is **(6)** _____, our brain releases chemicals that   QUALIFY

cause us to cheer for our mates or scream at the television, the sports

(7) _____, the person sitting next to us, and most often times, the   COMMENT

umpire or **(8)** _____. Even before a match, the brain chemicals released   REFER

into our bodies **(9)** _____ our senses as we prepare to watch the game.   SHARP

There's no denying some people their love of sport, and sometimes it's more

(10) _____ to watch a sports lover's reaction to sporting events than   CAPTIVATE

the actual event!

D Complete the text by writing one word in each gap.

Exploring Mars

Will we ever send a person to Mars? Although we don't know what the future **(1)** _____ , scientists
are of **(2)** _____ opinion that this will happen one day. Mars is certainly **(3)** _____
in line for human exploration, **(4)** _____ that so much effort has been put into sending
devices there so **(5)** _____ to learn more about it. An important factor **(6)** _____
exploring Mars is getting astronauts there safely. The recent landing of the Mars rover, Curiosity, is one source
(7) _____ inspiration that this is possible. The mission got **(8)** _____ to a good start.
Everything the scientists had been working **(9)** _____ paid off, **(10)** _____ the rover
landed successfully owing **(11)** _____ the home team responsible for guiding it there. It was a
smooth landing **(12)** _____ though there had been concerns about the mission, and the event was
(13) _____ momentous it made world headlines. In **(14)** _____ of all this progress, it
will be years before mankind travels there. For the time **(15)** _____ , we will simply have to explore it
from home.

E Think of one word only that can be used appropriately in all three sentences.

1 The choices we make early in life do a lot to _____ our future.

His behaviour is out of control and he really needs to _____ up.

Harry joined a gym so he could get in good _____.

2 Don't tell Margie about the surprise party; she can't keep a _____.

The fact that ordinary people can now travel into space is no state _____.

The meeting was held in _____ and I can't say what it was about.

3 She was doing so well until she _____ back to eighth place.

I would be disappointed with you if you _____ out of the race.

The project's success depended on Sarah, but unfortunately she _____ the ball.

4 Mark spilt water on the floor and the puppy tried to _____ it up.

It would a tragedy to give up during the last _____ of the race.

Marcy had gotten too big to sit on her mother's _____.

5 Hanna was set to win the match and nothing could _____ her back.

The team is very competitive and they _____ the record in the relay race.

The bars in the gymnastic wheel help you to _____ onto it.

F Complete the second sentences so that they have a similar meaning to the first sentences using the words in bold. Use between three and six words.

1 Both George and Paul are unprepared for the game.

NOR

_____ is ready for the game.

2 After Mike failed at the initial phase, he quit the project.

HURDLE

At the start of the project, Mike _____ and quit.

3 Mary said, 'I'm sorry I didn't make it to the game.'

FOR

Mary _____ the game.

4 The coach asked Henry, 'Did you practise this weekend?'

IF

The coach asked Harry _____ weekend.

5 'I'm so happy for your win!' Monica said to Karen.

CONGRATULATED

Monica _____ win.

6 Margaret received lots of money when she signed with the team.

KILLING

Margaret _____ the team.

7 Becoming a rocket scientist is the greatest thing after travelling in space.

NOTHING

_____ would be better than becoming a rocket scientist.

8 'Shall we watch the launch tomorrow?' Jill said to Oliver.

FOLLOWING

Jill asked Oliver if they _____ day.